Katharine Gibbs

Handbook of
Business English

Katharine Gibbs
Handbook of Business English

SECOND EDITION

Deborah Naclerio

an imprint of
K-III Reference Corporation
A K-III Communications Corporation company

Copyright © 1996 by Katharine Gibbs Schools, Inc.

A K-III Communications Corporation company

Katharine Gibbs Schools, Inc.
52 Vanderbilt Avenue
New York, New York 10017

Library of Congress Catalog Card Number: 82-48356

Printed in the United States of America

10 9 8 7 6 5 4 3 2 1

Library of Congress Cataloging in Publication Data

Main entry under title:
Katharine Gibbs handbook of business English.

    Includes index.
    1. English language——Grammar——1950-   2. English
language——Usage.   3. Commercial correspondence.
I. Katharine Gibbs Schools.
PE1112.K3 1982   808' .066651   82-48356
ISBN 0-8343-0106-7

Table of Contents

Foreword

The business training that will prove a recognized password into the business field must be more than facility with notebook and type-writer; it must represent a working knowledge of the principles and practices of modern business and professional life.

> Katharine M. Gibbs
> Founder
> Katharine Gibbs Schools

Katharine Gibbs wrote these words in 1922...words that still guide the educational principles at the Katharine Gibbs schools today. Thousands of students benefit from the many Gibbs programs through business programs that have, since 1911, helped to launch many notable careers.

Although "notebook and typewriter" may have been replaced by transcribers and personal computers, the need to understand and apply the important principles of proper English usage remains a cornerstone of the Katharine Gibbs English curriculum.

"Modern business" today, just as in past years, requires a sound mastery of the English language through a complete understanding of its rules and proper application. Use of language in its correct form is a valuable asset that carries with it a lifetime benefit.

Programs at any of the Gibbs schools provide the best opportunity to master English usage as well as today's "modern" skills. The Katharine Gibbs Handbook of Business English is an invaluable tool as a reference guide to proper English usage whether used within the Gibbs' lecture halls, computer labs, or in a business setting.

I invite you to use this handbook; it will help you obtain a mastery of language, which is a powerful tool that will improve your English skills and provide a significant advantage to you.

> William S. Kalaboke
> President and
> Chief Executive Officer
> Katharine Gibbs Schools, Inc.

Katharine Gibbs Schools, Inc.
Headquarters
52 Vanderbilt Avenue
New York, NY 10017

Preface

Over the years business people have consistently telephoned the Katharine Gibbs School nearest their offices to ask an "English question." How to choose between who and whom, when to capitalize a title, how to form a possessive in the name of an organization or publication, how to address a female minister—these are just a few of the problems that confront the careful writer on any level. Students, as well as those already experienced in the business world, have expressed the need for a book written in clear, simple language that incorporates the correct and current rules of style, grammar, punctuation, and usage. The Katharine Gibbs Handbook of Business English is such a book, giving clear, detailed coverage of each of these topics.

This revision of the 1982 edition of the Handbook covers the content, mechanics, and format of nontechnical written business communication with attention to the latest usage and the most modern word processing techniques. The section on model letters has been expanded to give more examples of business correspondence. The writing section offers clear directions on the latest trends of business writing without sacrificing any of the quality and correctness that have always been associated with the Gibbs name. The dictionary used in preparing this Handbook is *Webster's New World Dictionary*, Third College Edition.

The author gratefully acknowledges the confidence and support of Antoinette Ingulli, Vice-President of Education for the Katharine Gibbs Schools; the editorial expertise of Eugene Ehrlich, CARRUTH & EHRLICH BOOKS, INC.; the efforts of Joyce Maher, author of the companion workbook; and the suggestions, recommendations, and guidance of so many in the Gibbs schools—the faculties in Boston, Massachusetts, and Norwalk Connecticut; Nancy Makso, New York, New York; Joyce Gold, Montclair, New Jersey; Mary Sheridan, Piscataway, New Jersey; and especially Susan Masserwick and Theresa Messina, Melville, New York, and Ann Rodrigues, Providence, Rhode Island. I am especially grateful for the patience and understanding of family and friends, most notably my husband Frank and my sons Matthew and Michael, who cheerfully coped with cold meals and no laundry and my taking the computer on vacation!

Katharine Gibbs School
126 Newbury Street
Boston, Massachusetts 02116

Katharine Gibbs School
142 East Avenue
Norwalk, Connecticut 06851

Katharine Gibbs School
535 Broad Hollow Road
Melville, New York 11747

Katharine Gibbs School
80 Kingsbridge Road
Piscataway, New Jersey 08854

Katharine Gibbs School
33 Plymouth Street
Montclair, New Jersey 07042

Katharine Gibbs School
178 Butler Avenue
Providence, Rhode Island 02906

Katharine Gibbs School
200 Park Avenue
New York, New York 10166

CHAPTER 1

Style

Capitalization
Numbers
Abbreviations

Capitalization

Most writers agree upon the basic rules of capitalization. This is not true, however, of special rules. Individuals, organizations, and circumstances often demand variations from conventional style. The current trend in business writing is to

- Use capital letters sparingly
- Follow your company's preferences
- Be consistent within a text

Basic Rules

1. Capitalize the first word of every sentence.

> He said he would have no difficulty completing the project.
> The meeting was long but accomplished much.

2. Capitalize the pronoun *I*.

> She suggested that *I* apply for the position.

3. Capitalize all proper nouns and proper adjectives. (A proper noun is the name of a *particular* person, place, or thing. Well-known nicknames and descriptive names are also proper nouns.) Abbreviated forms of proper nouns and adjectives are also capitalized.

Proper Noun	Proper Adjective
Italy	Italian language
America	American history
Canada	Canadian province
Socrates	the Socratic method
Pulitzer Prize	Jacksonian democracy
Congressional Medal of Honor	
Wednesday	
Wed.	

Proper Noun	Descriptive Name/ Nickname
Abraham Lincoln	Honest Abe
the Rocky Mountains	the Rockies
New York City	the Big Apple
Europe	the Continent
Rome	the Eternal City
New Jersey	the Garden State
Linden Street	Uncle Sam

USING THE DICTIONARY: Many proper nouns and adjectives are listed in alphabetical order within the main text. When a word is capitalized in all its uses, the entry word itself is printed with a capital letter.

If a capitalized main-entry word has a use or uses that are uncapitalized, these are marked with a small-boldface, lowercase letter followed by a short dash and enclosed in brackets.

If a lowercase main-entry word has a use that requires a capital, this is marked with a boldface capital letter followed by a short dash and enclosed in brackets.

These entries are sometimes qualified by such self-explanatory terms as *often* , *usually,* *also,* or *occas.*

> European
> Puritan n...1...2[p-]...-adj.1...2[p-]
> north n...1...2...3...4[*often* N-]

4. Follow the individual preference of a person, organization, or publication when writing a name. (Ask directly, or follow letterhead stationery or company literature.)

> Texaco Inc.   Dewey & Dykeman   R. L. Haldeman
> Charles T. Smith, Jr.   Carlos de la Cruz   Hermann VanDerVeer
> Higgins and Higgins   the Xerox Corporation

Special Rules

Special rules govern the use of capitals in the following cases: (Remember, an individual company may have its own preferences)

Academic Degrees. Capitalize a degree used after a proper noun but not as a general term of classification.

> Roger Trettien, Ph.D.
> After she gets her bachelor of arts degree, she will work on her master's.

Addresses
Street Addresses. Capitalize and spell out all important words in a street address including words like Avenue, Street, Lane, Road.

> Please mail the completed form to 10 Linden Road in Walden.
> His office is at 416 Avenue of the Americas.

Cities and Towns. Capitalize and write out the name in full including words like Fort, Mount, Point, and Port. Abbreviate the word Saint (St.) only when the abbreviation is actually written that way in the geographical name.

> Mount Kisco   Fort Lee   St. Louis   St. Petersburg

State. For a mailing address use the two-letter ZIP Code abbreviation written in capitals and without periods. When not giving a specific mailing address, write the name of the state in full with an initial capital.

> She attended the Katharine Gibbs School in Norwalk, Connecticut.

Please mail the booklets to the following address:
5739 Carle Place
Houston, TX 77035

Brand Names and Trademarks.   Capitalize a brand name but not the common noun that follows it.

Xerox	Kleenex	Campbell soup	Ford cars
Vaseline	Coca-Cola	Lux soap	Crest toothpaste

Through popular usage certain words originally derived from proper nouns have lost their specialized meaning and are often not capitalized. When in doubt, consult a reliable, up-to-date dictionary.

manila paper	mimeograph	venetian blinds	nylon
aspirin	morocco leather	guinea hen	pasteurized milk

Buildings, Monuments, and Landmarks.   Capitalize the names of buildings, monuments, and landmarks but not the common noun when used alone, even in a specific reference, or when it is written in the plural following two or more proper nouns.

While in New York, I visited the Chrysler Building and the Empire State Building. These buildings...

While in New York, I visited the Chrysler and the Empire State buildings. These buildings...

On the students' itineraries are the Statue of Liberty and Grant's Tomb. These monuments are...

Calendar Terms.   Capitalize the names of holidays, holy days, days of the week, months of the year. Capitalize such words as day and week only when they are part of the name of a holiday. Do not capitalize the names of seasons unless they are personified in poetry or literature. Pay attention to the way apostrophes are used in these proper nouns.

National Secretaries' Week	Labor Day
New Year's Eve	Veterans Day
Washington's Birthday	Monday
September	Yom Kippur
Martin Luther King Day	Ramadan
in the fall	summer vacation

Courses of Study.   Capitalize the names of languages and specific course titles. Do <u>not</u> capitalize general areas of study: biology, history, and so forth.

He failed French but passed sociology.

My favorite English course is The Victorian Poets.

Because I love biology and history, I registered for Biology 201 and Modern American History.

4

Direct Address. Capitalize names and titles used in direct address. Do not capitalize the words *madam, sir, ladies, gentlemen,* and *miss* when used alone in direct address.

> I assure you, gentlemen, we will meet the deadline.

> Dr. Cortez, your appointment as adjunct lecturer has been unanimously confirmed.

> Yes, Professor, my assignment is complete.

First Words. In addition to the first word in every sentence, capitalize the first word of...

An independent clause following a colon.

> Our store has one policy: The customer is always right.

An independent clause within quotation marks. When the source interrupts the quotation, only the first word of the sentence is capitalized.

> He closed by saying, "Everything else is irrelevant."
> "Everything else," he said, "is irrelevant."

An independent question inserted in a sentence.

> We discussed the question Do we really need a new library? at last night's meeting.

Each item in a tabulated list or an outline.

> Television Today   He made these proposals:
>   I. Introduction   1. That all members be invited.
>   II. Programs   2. That the minutes be accepted.
>   III. Commercials   3. That dues be increased.
>   IV. Conclusion

A sentence enclosed in parentheses <u>not</u> inside another sentence. If the parenthetic sentence is within another sentence, capitalize the first word only if it is a proper noun or other word ordinarily capitalized.

> I have enclosed the catalog you requested. (The price list is on page 21.)

> I have enclosed a catalog (the price list is on page 21) that lists all the articles in which you showed interest.

> The personnel manager needs the health insurance form (I enclose two copies) by Wednesday.

The first word of the subtitle of a book, even when the word is not normally capitalized.

> *The Journey Home: A Voyage of Self-Discovery*

Historical Events and Periods. Capitalize the names of historical events and time periods.

the Boston Tea Party	Prohibition	the Middle Ages
the American Revolution	the Victorian Era	World War II
the Gay Nineties		the Roaring Twenties

Do not capitalize undescribed decades and centuries.

the mid-sixties	the nineteenth century

Hyphenated Words. Capitalize proper nouns and proper adjectives in hyphenated compounds.

the East-West games	American-Italian relations
the Gramm-Rudman Act	Marxist-Leninist theories

Do not capitalize a prefix or suffix joined to a proper noun or adjective except in a heading or title.

ex-President Carter	President-elect Mason
post-World War II	*Life in Post-Elizabethan England*

Do not capitalize common nouns joined to proper nouns except in a title or heading.

an Ohio-based company
English-speaking people
the book *English Among English-Speaking People*

Laws and Treaties. Capitalize official and accepted titles of laws, amendments, treaties, bills, and so forth.

Do not capitalize the common noun even in specific reference. Exception: The word *Constitution* is capitalized when referring to the Constitution of the United States.

Social Security Act. . .that act. . .
the Nineteenth Amendment. . .the amendment. . .
the Treaty of Versailles. . .the treaty. . .

Medical Terms. Many medical terms include the name of the person who discovered the disease, test, drug, and so forth. These and other proper nouns that are part of medical terminology are capitalized; common nouns are lowercased. Generic names of drugs are lowercased; trade names are capitalized

Alzheimer's disease	German measles	Parkinson's disease
herpes simplex	Ritalin	methylphenidate

Numbers and Letters for Identification. When you identify an object by giving it a number or letter, the letter is always capitalized. The preceding noun or nouns are capitalized. Exceptions: *page, paragraph, line, sentence,* and *verse,* for which capitalization is optional.

Conference Room A	Gate 6	Page 27 or page 27	Chapter 11

Organizations.   Capitalize all important words in the full name of all organizations (business, civic, educational, governmental, political, professional, religious, and social). Do not capitalize *a, an, the;* prepositions of fewer than five letters; or the conjunctions *and, or, but, nor.*

> the Democratic Party   the Sons of Italy
> Sony Corporation of America   the Rockefeller Foundation
> the University of Maryland   St. Luke's Episcopal Church
> the American Society of University Professors
> the Savings and Loan Association of Minneapolis

Capitalize the article *the* before a title when it is part of the official name of the organization. Check the letterhead to be sure.

> *The New York Times*   *The Wall Street Journal*

Always verify the style preference of an organization with regard to capitalization, spelling, punctuation, abbreviations, and the use of use of ampersands.

> Lord & Taylor's   Macmillan Publishing Co., Inc.

If you use the common noun at the end of the organization name in place of the full name, do not capitalize it. Such words include *association, board, college, club, board, committee, company, corporation, league,* and *university.*

> She attends Manhattanville College in New York. The college offers an
> excellent liberal arts program.

In some formal documents such as an annual report or legal contract or within an organization itself, use capitals when the full name has already been given and the article *the* precedes the word.

> We have officially approved the enclosed policy for the Mobil Oil Credit
> Corporation. This agreement will enable *the Corporation* to limit its liability.

> The Tucson City Women's Club convened on March 22. The Club members
> unanimously approved the minutes of the previous meeting.

Departments.   Capitalize a department or division name on an envelope, in the inside address, and in the signature block. It is important to follow company style in these matters.

> Frampton Educational Company
> A Division of Frampton Publishing, Inc.

Within a sentence the department or division name is not usually capitalized except by the employees of the organization or in the shortened form of the name. It is important to follow company style in these matters.

> I have already checked these facts with Ms. Lee in Accounting.

> The Personnel Department will handle all interviews for secretarial positions
> opening up this month. (Interoffice Memorandum)

> Please get me the name of the head of the personnel department of the
> company that provides trash collection for us.

Government Agencies. Capitalize the words *federal, government, national,* and *court* only when part of an official name.

> National Security Council
> Federal Bureau of Investigation
> the Supreme Court
> United States Government Printing Office

> In the national interest. . .
> Many federal regulations. . .
> All government agencies. . .

> By next month the court will rule. . .
> federal, state, and local laws
> the federal government

Parts of a Letter

Salutation. Capitalize the first word and all nouns and titles.

> Dear Mrs. Karges: Dear Professor Juarez:

Complimentary Close. Capitalize the first word only.

> Sincerely yours,   Very truly yours,

Envelope, inside and return addresses, signature block. Capitalize all names and titles.

> Mr. John Delaney, President
> Mr. John Delaney
> Chairman of the Board

Attention and Subject lines. Capitalize the first word and all important words. Do not capitalize articles, conjunctions, or prepositions of fewer than five letters.

> ATTENTION: Mrs. Julia Collard, President
> SUBJECT: Quarterly Sales Reports

In care of. Spell out with an initial cap. You may use c/o to save space.

> Miss Barbara Wydell
> In care of Ms. Louise Craig

> Ms. Louise Craig
> c/o Mr. Bartholomew Wiggins-Craig

Place Names. Capitalize parts of the world or regions of a continent or country.

> Europe   the Middle East
> the Atlantic Ocean   the Atlantic
> Tropic of Cancer   the Tropics
> the Continent   the Pacific Rim

Do not capitalize descriptive adjectives not specifically part of the place name.

| southern New York | out West | upper Louisiana |

Capitalize popular descriptive names of specific regions and localities.

the Deep South	Wall Street
the Great Plains	the Loop
Chinatown (New York)	Back Bay (Boston)
the Sunbelt	the City of Brotherly Love (Philadelphia)
the Lower East Side	the Upper West Side

Capitalize *North, South, East, West*, and *Central* only when used as names of large, well-known regions of the world or the United States (always preceded by *the*). These words are not capitalized as adjectives or nouns when referring to directions or not part of a commonly accepted proper noun.

the East	the South	the Midwest
the East Coast	the Northwest	South American
South Dakota	Central America	Southeast Asia
eastern Nebraska	the Southern Hemisphere	northern New Jersey

The South was devastated after the Civil War.
The prevailing wind is from the south.

However...

He is proud to be a Midwesterner (Southerner, Northerner, etc.).
The inn is famous for its Southern hospitality.

Political Divisions. Capitalize words designating national, regional, or local political divisions when they follow a place name and are an official part of it.

| Washington State | Kansas City | Fairfield County |

Lowercase such words as *city, state,* and *county* when they precede a proper noun and are not used as part of an official name.

The city of New York comprises five boroughs.
The delegates from the state of Maine have not arrived.

Other Geographical Locations. Capitalize the names of mountains, lakes, rivers, islands, and so forth. A generic topographical term (mountain, lake, island) used as part of the name is also capitalized but is not capped when used alone.

Narragansett Bay	the bay
Rocky Mountains	the mountains
Amazon River	the river
the Philippine Islands	the islands
Lakes Huron and Erie	the lakes
the Ohio and Mississippi Valleys	the valleys
Westchester and Fairfield counties	the counties

Religious Terms. Names of religions, denominations, creeds, religious orders, prayers, sacred books, and well-known passages of the Bible are capitalized. When in doubt, consult your dictionary.

Ten Commandments	Catholic
the Society of Jesus	the Lord's Prayer
Old Testament	the Southern Baptist Convention
Koran	the Talmud

Special Words, Mottoes, Sayings. Capitalize references within a sentence to notations on bills, letters, packages, and signs. These notations are often used with such words as *labeled*, *marked*, and *stamped*. Capitalize the first word of commonly known mottoes and sayings. All of these are also enclosed in quotation marks.

> Someone stamped "Paid" on the attached bill.
> He posted a "No Smoking" sign in each office.
> The most important rule is "When in doubt, spell it out."
> His favorite saying is "Honesty is the best policy."

Time Zones. Capitalize time zones. When using an abbreviation, type in full caps with no spaces and no periods.

Eastern Standard Time	EST
Central Standard Time	CST
Pacific Standard Time	PST

The term *daylight saving time* (also *daylight savings time*) is usually written without capitals.

Titles of Persons. Capitalize titles of honor, position, and public office when the title precedes a name unless the name is in apposition and is set off by commas.

Miss Norma Fishburn	Vice-President Coburn
Professor Rubriz	Dr. Sung
Ambassador Hamlin	Colonel Newman
Rabbi Weinberg	the Reverend Michael Bailey

> I spoke to Dean Marcus at the ceremony.
> I spoke to the dean, James Marcus, at the ceremony.

This rule also applies to family relationships.

> Give this package to your uncle.   I gave it to Uncle Henry.

Always capitalize the titles of high-ranking officials whether the title precedes, follows, or is used in place of the person's name. General references, however, are not capitalized. All references to the President of the United States are capitalized.

> While in Rome, I had an audience with the Pope.
> The Prime Minister of England visited Canada last year.
> The Secretary of Defense met with the President at noon.
> I had asked to speak with the Governor of Iowa, but any governor could have answered my questions.

Other titles used alone, after, or in place of a name are usually not capitalized unless the writer wishes to show special respect or importance, usually within an organization or in a local publication.

> She is dean of students at Colby College.
> Mr. Wilcox, chairman of the board, is in his office.
> Ms. Garcia, Dean of Secretarial Studies, ... (within an organization)

Ex-, *-elect*, *former*, and *late* are not capitalized even if the title is.

> President-elect Johnson will preside at tomorrow's meeting.

Titles of Works.   Capitalize the first word, the last word, and all other important words in the titles of publications, broadcasts, works of art, reports, plays, lectures, and so forth.

Do not capitalize articles, conjunctions, or prepositions of fewer than five letters.

Capitalize *the* only if it is part of the official title.

When naming something that is part of a collection or a larger whole—for example, a chapter in a book— put the title in quotation marks. Otherwise, titles are italicized. If italics are unavailable, underscore may be used.

Books:	*The American West; Modern Business English*
Magazines:	*Newsweek; U. S. News & World Report*
Newspapers:	*The New York Times; The Chicago Tribune*
Columns:	"Wall Street Analysis"
Chapters:	"Building Self-Esteem"
Articles:	"Planning for Your Retirement"
Reports:	*Problems of the Four-Day Workweek*
Television Programs:	*Sixty Minutes; Murder She Wrote*
Television Episode:	"The Case of the Weeping Widow"
Movie:	*The Silence of the Lambs*
Plays:	*My Fair Lady*
Works of Art:	Michelangelo's *Pieta*
Songs:	"Moon River"
Major musical works:	*Messiah, La Bohème*
Poems:	"The Death of the Hired Man"
Major poetical works:	*The Canterbury Tales*
Ships:	*Titanic*
Trains:	*Cannonball Express*
Aircraft:	*Songbird*
Spacecraft:	*Explorer I*
Speeches:	"The Road Ahead"
Radio Program:	*Great Masterworks*
Radio Episode:	"The United Nations—History and Future"

Quick Study

Capitalize

...all proper **nouns** and **adjectives**

Sarah Smith	the Chrysler Building	the Mississippi River
New Year's Day	the Middle Ages	Eastern Standard Time
the Koran	Parkinson's disease	Washington State
the Garden State	Jericho Turnpike	Italian-American citizens
J. D. Blake, Jr.	First Methodist Church	National Education Week

...specific references to all **governments** and **titles of government officials**

Great Britain	the Secretary of State	Social Security Act
the President-elect	District Attorney Jones	House of Representatives
the Supreme Court	U.S. Senate	the 21st Amendment

...**large sections of a country** or the world but not directions

West Virginia	drove north on Route 9	lived in the Midwest
southern Vermont	South Korea	the Southern Hemisphere

...**titles before names** but not in other positions except for government officials or to show special respect

Dean John Smith	saw the Pope	the Governor will speak
our vice-president	the Secretary of Defense	Laura Smith, dean of students

...**trade names** but not the common noun that follows

Lux soap	Xerox copier	Kleenex tissues

...**languages** and **course titles** but not general subjects

speaks Italian	English-speaking persons
Biology 101	likes to read history

...important words in **addresses**

Miss Alice Vanderbilt
Assistant Treasurer
Accounting Department
10 East 36th Street
New York, NY 10017

...**nouns** before numbers or letters in sequence

Room 401	Style No. 1106

...the **first word** and **all important words** in organization names and in the titles of books, plays, articles, songs, and so forth. Do not capitalize articles, conjunctions, or prepositions of fewer than five letters.

In general, **italicize** titles of books, newspapers, magazines, movies, plays, reports, television and radio shows, works of art, and major musical and poetical works.

Use **quotes** for short stories, poems, chapters or sections in a publication, columns, one episode of a radio or television program, and songs.

The Wall Street Journal	*Sixty Minutes*
Newsweek	*Windsong: A Cat's Tale* (BOOK)
Handel's *Messiah*	*The Canterbury Tales*
"Trees" (POEM)	"Moon River" (song)
Pieta	"Wall Street Analysis" (COLUMN)
Personnel Policies (REPORT)	

...the **first word** of a sentence and of a sentence after a colon

> One thing is clear: We must increase our staff.

...the **first word** of a complete sentence in quotes

> Mr. Cortinez said, "We must increase our staff."

...the **first word** of an independent question inserted in a sentence.

> The question Who is retiring? did not come up.

...the **first word** of a full sentence in parentheses if not inside another sentence.

> I have enclosed the spring catalog. (The price list is on page 22.)
> The enclosed catalog (the price list is on page 22) will help you select the items you need.

...each element in a **tabulation** or outline

> The following items were discussed:
> 1. Wages
> 2. Vacation days
> 3. Raises

Numbers

Numbers are an essential part of every business communication. Every business letter includes, at the very least, the numbers in the date and in the addresses. Time, measurements, prices—all are common parts of a business message. A number expressed ambiguously or incorrectly may result in a costly misunderstanding.

In general, write numbers in a style appropriate to their context. Following are the three basic styles of expressing numbers in business writing:

Formal Style

A graduation, a state dinner, an official announcement or proclamation—these are all formal occasions, requiring formal writing. In addition, high-level executive correspondence may use the formal style of expressing numbers to avoid giving them unintended emphasis. In formal writing numbers are usually spelled out.

Technical Style

Many businesses are involved in communicating technical information. Engineering and architectural firms, medical laboratories, and many other organizations use numbers in countless situations. In technical writing, numbers are expressed in figures.

Nontechnical Business Style

Business correspondence can certainly contain technical references. It can also be intentionally formal. The more formal the style, the less frequently will figures appear.

Most contemporary writers agree that numbers expressed in figures are easier and faster to read. However, the ordinary business letter, memorandum, or report will observe the following rules of nontechnical business English:

A sentence must begin with words, not figures; so always spell out a number at the beginning of a sentence or rephrase the sentence so that the number falls within it.

> Ten thousand copies were printed in June.
> In June we printed 10,000 copies.

If no special rule applies...

Spell out numbers under 10 and numbers not worthy of special emphasis.

> The contract has been in effect for seven years.

(When spelled out, numbers expressed in two words between *twenty-one* and *ninety-nine* are hyphenated.)

Write numbers in figures starting with 10 and all numbers worthy of emphasis.

> The warehouse has shipped 12 cartons.

Be consistent. Having decided how to express a particular number, adhere to that style throughout a given text.

Special Rules

Abbreviations. Always use figures with abbreviations. (Although abbreviations seldom appear in non-technical business writing, an occasional technical reference may require their use.) In addition, except at the beginning of a sentence, use *No.* for number and *Nos.* for numbers.

> She ordered Nos. 14 and 15.
> Number 23 is missing.
> She used 35-mm film.
> He sold Model No. 377.

Addresses. Use figures for all house and building numbers. Write out avenue and street numbers less than 10. Use figures for those 10 and greater. Always use the ordinal endings *st, th, nd (or d),* and *rd (or d).*

1 First Avenue	10 Main Street	2 Lexington Avenue
6 East Fourth Street	12 East 54th Street	1190 102nd Street

Acceptable Variations: All street and avenue names through Ninety-ninth Street or Avenue may be spelled out. The word *One* may be used for a house or building number.

> One Park Avenue   16 Twelfth Street

ZIP Codes are written in figures without commas. They are typed a single space after the state when they are part of an address within a sentence.

> She lives at 6399 Lakeland Avenue, El Toro, CA 92630.

In an address that appears on an envelope or is set off within a letter, use a double space between the state and the ZIP Code.

> Please forward this order to me at the following address:
> 6399 Lakeland Avenue
> El Toro, CA 92630-9576

Advertising and Sales. For quick reading, easy comprehension, and emphasis, numbers in sales writing and advertising are almost always expressed in figures.

> At Kramer's you can buy 2 for the price of 1!

Ages. Express the ages of people and animals in figures.

> At 25 years of age, Julia Vasquez is the youngest candidate.

> a 7-year-old boy   a 3 1/2-year-old child
> in his 60s   a class for 4-year-olds

For ages of inanimate objects and other things, spell out numbers under 10; use figures for those 10 and up.

> a two-year fight   The house is 11 years old.
> our five-year plan   the 40-year-old building

In an expression of age that includes months and days, always use figures; omit internal punctuation.

> He gave his age as 50 years 6 months 13 days.

Anniversaries. In general, write out ordinal numbers (first, second, third, fiftieth) used to enumerate anniversaries.

> Shortly after their fifteenth anniversary, the Wilsons bought this house.

Use figures when more than two words are needed

> In the year 2001 our country will celebrate its 225th anniversary.

Use figures when special emphasis is desired.

> Your 50th anniversary will be a memorable occasion.

Consecutive Numbers. When two numbers that are written in the same style come together in a sentence, use a comma to separate them.

> Of the seven, two were disqualified.
> In 1990, 200 workers went on strike.

When two numbers come together in a sentence and one is part of a compound modifier, write out the first number unless the second number is significantly shorter. Since the two numbers are written in different styles, no comma is necessary.

> She bought twelve 32-cent stamps.
> She bought 200 three-cent stamps.

Credit Terms. Numbers in credit terms are expressed in figures.

> Their terms were 2 percent 10 days, net 30 days.

Dates. Use cardinal figures (1,2,3, and so forth) when the date follows the month.

> on June 2   on Tuesday, June 22, ...

Use either ordinal numbers (first, second, and so forth) or figures with ordinal endings (1st, 2nd, 3rd, and so forth) when the date appears after the word *the*.

> on the 2nd of June   on the second of June
> since the third   since the 22nd of last month

A comma is required after the year in a date-year combination. If just the month and year are given, however, no punctuation is required.

> On June 2, 1995, we...   in June 1995
> ...on June 2, 1995.   in June of 1995

Foreign or military correspondence usually shows the date as a cardinal figure written before the month and year without commas.

> on 2 June l995

Decimals. Numbers with decimals are expressed in figures. To prevent misreading, place a zero before a decimal that does not have a whole number unless the decimal itself begins with a zero.

> He found a discrepancy of 0.3 percent.
> Her measurement was .004 inch shorter than mine.
> We had 22.25 inches of snow in January.

> EXCEPTION: The store sells .22 caliber rifles.

Enumerations. Numbers in parentheses are sometimes used in run-on enumerations.

> A tenant usually must (1) pay all rent due on the first of the month, (2) keep the premises clean and undamaged, and (3) pay utility bills on time.

Fractions. Spell out single-digit denominator fractions. Hyphenate all spelled-out fractions.

> She waited one-half hour.
> She covered three-fourths of the lesson.
> The price has increased one-half cent.
> We can use a three-eighth-inch strip.
> He gave his agent one-fourth of his income.

Use figures for double-digit (or more) denominator fractions.

> 1/10   3/16   5/125

> We need only a 7/10-inch piece.
> The molding is 3/16 of an inch short.

Use figures for mixed figures (a whole number plus a fraction).

7 1/2 inches   12 3/4 feet

Do not mix fractions that appear on the keyboard with those that do not. Leave one space between a whole number and a fraction; leave no space before or after the diagonal bar.

The room is exactly 27 3/4 feet long.

Indefinite Numbers. Express indefinite numbers in words.

a few thousand students   cost them millions
hundreds of books   several million dollars

Law and Finance. In legal or financial correspondence and documents, express important numbers in words followed by confirming figures enclosed in parentheses.

A check for twenty-five thousand dollars ($25,000) will be deposited by the first of every month.

Military and Political Divisions, Religious Organizations, Churches. These proper nouns often contain ordinal numbers that are spelled out.

Third Congregational Church   Seventh-Day Adventists
the Third Reich   First Continental Congress
the Third Armored Battalion   The Sixteenth Congressional District

Money. Use figures for exact and approximate amounts beginning with 1 cent. Write out the word cent(s).

The price of steel rose only 50 cents a ton.

Use the dollar sign with exact and approximate amounts beginning with $1. Repeat the dollar sign before amounts in succession.

The dresses sell for $49.95 and $75.
The book costs about $20.

An even number of dollars is written without a decimal point and two zeros except in a tabulation that includes amounts expressed in dollars and cents.

He paid me $50 a week.   but $12.97
                                          20.00
                                           5.95

A sum of money may combine with one or more other words to form a one-thought modifier of a following noun. Hyphenate accordingly. Do <u>not</u> hyphenate the simple adjectival form.

a $50-a-week raise   He received $50 a week.
a 35-cent stamp   a $10 million loan
a one-half-cent increase 9 cents apiece

The words *cent(s)* and *dollar(s)* become possessive nouns <u>only</u> when followed by the word *worth*.

Five dollars' worth of supplies.   about 2 cents' worth

When a sum of money expressed with a dollar sign precedes *worth*, no possession is shown.

He bought $5 worth of supplies.

Sums of money in round numbers with seven or more digits may be expressed in three ways. The first column is preferred.

$1 million	1 million dollars	$1,000,000
$25 billion	25 billion dollars	$25,000,000,000
$3.2 million	3.2 million dollars	$3,200,000

Repeat the word and the $ if using more than one sum in a sentence.

The budget for the project was cut from $6 million to $3 million.

Express related amounts of money the same way.

...from $750,000 to $1,000,000. (not $1 million)

Foreign Money. Pounds and pennies (in Great Britain formerly called *pence*) use symbols. Other foreign currencies are expressed with a number and a word.

9 francs	50 pesos	25,000 lire
a halfpenny	8.75£	35 centavos

Numbers as Numbers. When referring to a number as a number, write it in figures. Do not underscore or italicize the figure.

Many people consider 7 a lucky number.

Numbers for Identification. When you identify an object by giving it a number, the number is always written in figures. The preceding noun or nouns are always capitalized.

She will meet us at Gate 6.
The meeting will be held in Conference Room 12.

Long numbers for identification are usually written without commas. Some, however, may be written with hyphens, spaces, commas, or other devices to make them easier to read. In all cases follow the style of your source.

Page 1482	Style 2730
Invoice No. 34567	Social Security No. 562-07-6798
Model H-0245	License No. RT 098 785
Lot 75/354	Patent No. 976,089

Capitalization of the words *line, sentence, verse, paragraph,* and *page* is optional before a number.

Page 89   or   page 89

Outlines.   Outlines often use Roman numerals, Arabic numerals, and letters.

      I.   Editorial Tasks
             A. Manuscript editing
             B. Author contact
                 1. Authors under contract
                 2. New authors
      II.   Production Responsibilities
             A. Scheduling
                 1. Composition
                 2. Printing and binding
             B. Cost estimates and bids
                 1. Composition
                 2. Printing and Binding
                    a.
                    b.
                        (1)
                        (2)
                            (a)
                            (b)

Percents.   Use figures starting with 1 percent. Do not use the percent symbol (%) except in technical or statistical material. Never put a hyphen between the number and the word *percent*.

        a 2 percent increase   a 10 percent profit

Use decimals or follow the fraction rule for percentages less than 1.

        a 0.5 percent tax increase
        one-third percent lower than expected
        1/10 percent per kilowatt hour decrease
        a range of one-half to 1 percent
        7.5 percent or 7 1/2 percent

Do not use *percent* when *percentage point* is meant. For example, if 30-year fixed mortgages go from 10 to 11 percent, that is a rise of one percentage point, but an increase of 10 percent in the rates.

Ratio and Proportion.   Express ratios and proportions in figures.

        The proportion of flour to shortening is 3 to 1 in this recipe.

Related Numbers.   Numbers used in a similar way within a text should be expressed in the same way. If one is expressed in figures—that is, 10 or up—all must be expressed in figures.

        Of the 70 students in the class, only 5 went to the math fair.
        We bake cakes to serve 8, 25, or 50 people.
        We will have timings of 5, 10, and 15 minutes.
        The monorail comes at intervals of either five or eight minutes.

The fact that a number at the beginning of a sentence must be written as a word does not affect the expression of the numbers that follow.

> Five of the 70 students in the class went to the math fair.

Unrelated numbers follow their own rules.

> The 12 committee members were given five more days to complete the project. The nine volunteers all said they expect to come in under their budget of $500.

Roman Numerals.   Roman numerals are used for important divisions of literary and legislative material, in outlines, in dates on public buildings, and in proper names.

Volume III	World War II	Pope John XXIII
Chapter X	Part V	Queen Elizabeth II

Pages in the front section of a book or a formal report (such as the preface or table of contents) are usually numbered in lowercase Roman numerals: i, ii, iii, iv, v, and so forth. The body of the report is numbered in Arabic numerals starting with 1.

Symbols.   With the exception of the $, symbols (%, #, @, °) are used only in technical references. Do not use a symbol at the beginning of a sentence.

> We agree that $200 is a fair price.
> Two hundred dollars is a fair price.

Tabulations.   Numbers followed by a period are often used in a tabulation.

> The following are the tenant's responsibilities:
>
> 1. Pay all rent due on the first of the month.
> 2. Keep the premises clean and undamaged.
> 3. Pay all utility bills on time.

Telephone Numbers.   Telephone numbers are written in figures with the Area Code in parentheses followed by a space. Place a hyphen between the exchange and the individual number.

> (203) 555-1400

ACCEPTABLE VARIATIONS: Area Code 203 555-1400   or   1-203 555-1400.

Temperatures.   Temperatures are written in figures (except zero) with the word *degrees.* The use of the degree symbol (°) is acceptable in tables.

> 85 degrees   a drop of 9 degrees
> zero degrees   a 9-degree drop

The patient's temperature reached 101.9 degrees.

Time

Clock Time. Time may always be expressed in figures. Noon and midnight may be used alone or with the number 12. "On the hour" times in a sentence do not require the colon and two zeros (:00). The dictionary shows AM and PM as the first choice for these abbreviations, but A.M. and a.m., P.M. and p.m. are also considered acceptable.

at 8:30 PM	at 12 noon
at 9 AM	at midnight
at 8 o'clock	at 11:45

As with money, in tables use :00 when lining up "on the hour" times with those including minutes.

Avoid the redundant "AM in the morning," "PM in the evening, at night, and in the afternoon."

The meeting will begin at 8:30 in the morning. . . . or 8:30 AM.

ACCEPTABLE VARIATION: For a more formal style use words with o'clock or when AM or PM is omitted. Note: A hyphen is placed between the last two words.

eight o'clock	nine in the morning
nine-thirty o'clock	four forty-five in the afternoon

Special Years. Years with academic or historical significance may be expressed in abbreviated figures.

the Class of '90   the Spirit of '76

Decades should be expressed in figures. (Note: no apostrophe before the s)

the l990s   the '90s   the mid-'60s

ACCEPTABLE VARIATIONS: the Gay Nineties, the Roaring Twenties, the mid-sixties, the nineties.

Centuries should follow the 1 through 9 rule.   Hyphenate the adjectival form.

the first century	the 12th century	21st-century technology
the eighth century	the 20th century	a sixth-century ruin

Votes. Voting results should always be expressed in numbers.

The proposal was accepted 14 to 7.
The vote was 47 to 3 with 6 abstentions.
. . .a 25-to-17 vote. . .a 9-to-5 ruling.

Weights and Measures. All weights and measures are expressed in figures with the unit of measurement spelled out except in tabular or technical material.

A metric measurement of five or more figures is separated into groups of three with a single space, counting from right to left. A standard measurement of five or more figures is separated into groups of three with a comma, counting right to left. The comma in a four-digit number is optional.

12,900 people	$45,000	115,000
5 feet	25 inches	1,896 miles
1200 gallons	3 1/2 yards	1810 kilometers
1 foot taller	4 pints	1 quart

Hyphenate a number-word combination forming a one-thought modifier in front of a noun.

a 6-ton truck	an 8-foot wall	a 10-gallon hat

When the unit of measurement (inch, foot, and so forth) in two compounds is expressed only once, a hyphen followed by a space (a suspended hyphen) follows the first number.

a 3- by 5-inch card	5-, 10-, and 15-minute intervals
a 3-inch by 5-inch card	5-minute, 10-minute, and 15-minute intervals
a card 3 by 5 inches	intervals of 5, 10, and 15 minutes

When several words are needed to express the measurement, treat them as a unit, and do not use punctuation between the items.

This room is 10 yards 2 feet 8 inches in length.

Quick Study

Use figures for

Abbreviations	Style No. 21
Advertising and Sales	Buy 3. Get 1 free!
Ages of People	Jack Smith, 25
Credit terms	2 percent 10 days, net 30 days
Dates	June 2, the 2nd of June
Decades	the 1960s
Decimals	0.3 percent
Double-digit denominator fractions	3/16
House and Building Numbers	10 Park Avenue
Mixed Numbers	3 1/2
Money	$14.95, 5 cents, $1 million
Numbers as Numbers	Lucky 7
Numbers for Identification	Chapter 6
Percents of 1 and up	10 percent
Ratios	3 to 1
Telephone Numbers	(201) 546-9876
Temperatures except zero	76 degrees, zero degrees
Time	8:30 PM, 8 o'clock at night
Votes	14 to 7
Weights and Measures	75 pounds, 15 gallons, a 9-foot room
Year Dates	1976
Zip Codes	11030

Use words for

Anniversaries	Tenth Anniversary
Single-digit denominator fractions	one-half percent, gave me one fourth
Indefinite Numbers	a few million
Military and Political Divisions	Sixteenth Congressional District
Religious Organizations	Third Congregational Church
The beginning of a sentence	Thirty-two members were present.

Use words under 10, figures for 10 and greater.

Avenue and Street Numbers	2 East Fourth Street, 42nd Avenue
Ages of inanimate objects	our five-year plan, a building 12 years old
Centuries	ninth century, 20th century

Abbreviations

An abbreviation, the shortened form of a word or phrase, is generally limited to technical writing, statistical material, and material written in tables. Abbreviations occur frequently in such business documents as catalogs and standard forms, where the aim is to say the most in the least amount of space. Very formal writing will contain few, if any, abbreviations. For most types of business writing, use abbreviations sparingly.

Basic Rules

1. In any text always write out the expression in full first, followed by the abbreviation in parentheses:

> The United Arab Emirates (UAE) announced that...

In all subsequent references you may use the abbreviation alone.

> The UAE further announced. . .

2. Never begin a sentence with an abbreviation except for courtesy titles. (Mr., Mrs., Ms., Dr. and their respective plurals where applicable)

3. Be consistent within a given text. Do not abbreviate a word in some sentences and spell it out in others.

Using the Dictionary: *Webster's New World Dictionary* lists many abbreviations alphabetically in the text. Always check for the correct form or forms of an abbreviation. When a word can be abbreviated in more than one way, choose one and use it consistently.

The trend is toward less rather than more punctuation, so many abbreviations that were customarily written with periods no longer contain them. The dictionary shows very few abbreviations with periods as a first choice, although many are shown as second or third choices; however, since this practice does not seem to have taken hold in most of the business world, this text shows many abbreviations with periods. You may always eliminate the periods if your company approves.

Capitalization and Hyphenation of Abbreviations. Capitalize and hyphenate an abbreviated word exactly as you would were it written out in full.

January	Jan.	Company	Co.
foot-ton	ft-tn	Incorporated	Inc.

EXCEPTIONS:	B.C.	before Christ
	A.D.	anno Domini
	PTA	Parent-Teacher Association

Plurals of Abbreviations. See Plurals, Page 111.

Special Rules

Names and Titles

Personal Names. Always follow the person's own preference when writing a name, using initials or an abbreviation exactly the way he or she does. An initial is always followed by a period and a space.

> Chas. A. Smythe E. L. Doctorow J. Wilson Adams Marie St. James

Some people are known only by their initials, which are written without periods or spaces.

> FDR JFK LBJ

The abbreviations Jr. and Sr. are used only with a person's <u>full name</u>. The same is true of 2d (2nd), 3d (3rd), II, III.   A courtesy title may precede the name.

> Alan Blake Jr. Mr. Alan Blake Jr. **but not** Mr. Blake Jr.
> Harris L. Troy II Harris L. Troy 2d **but not** Mr. Troy II

A comma is not used before Jr. and Sr. or 2d and 3d or II and III unless the person prefers it. If a comma is used before any of these designations, the comma must also be used after it. The second comma is omitted when the name is made possessive.

> Warren B. Young, Jr., has invited us to speak at the committee meeting.
> Warren B. Young, III, has invited us to speak ...
>
> Warren B. Young, Jr.'s speech was very well received in Congress.
> Warren B. Young, III's speech was...

Titles. Always abbreviate a **courtesy title** when it precedes a person's full name or surname. Exception: Miss, Misses.

> Mr. John Blake Messrs. Hall and Blake
> Mrs. William Randall Mmes. Ryder and Randall
> Ms. Emily Andrews Mss. Andrews and LaRosa
> Miss Ann Romano Misses Romano and Trent

In general, spell out **other titles** used with personal names.

> Professor Adrianne Shapiro
> Senator J. Randall Wright

Use *Honorable*, capitalized and spelled out, before the full name (first name and/or initials and surname) or title of an elected or appointed government official. A title is often preceded by the article *the*, which is capitalized in an inside address or envelope address but not in a sentence.

> We are pleased to announce that the Honorable Mary F. Rogers will address our conference.

Using the abbreviation *Hon.* in an address or a table is acceptable though less formal.

Use *Reverend*, capitalized and spelled out, before the full name or title of a member of the clergy. It is often preceded by *the*, which is capitalized in an inside address or envelope address but not in a sentence.

> The speaker today is the Reverend Dr. Martha Opitz.
> The charity was founded by the Reverend Harris Blackford.

Using the abbreviation Rev. in an address or in tabular matter is acceptable though less formal.

The Reverend Harris K. Blackford		Rev. H. K. Blackford
1347 Hawthorne Avenue	**or**	1347 Hawthorne Avenue
Amityville, NY 10056		Amityville, NY 10056

Lengthy religious, military, and honorary titles should always be spelled out in formal correspondence but may be abbreviated in informal correspondence.

Brigadier General John Jones	Brig. Gen. John Jones
Lieutenant Commander Preston Smith	Lt. Comdr. Preston Smith
Right Reverend Monsignor Walter Wills	Rt. Rev. Monsignor Walter Wills

See pages 226-237 for the use of titles in addresses and for the use of titles in salutations.

Academic Degrees and Religious Orders. Although the dictionary shows virtually all academic abbreviations without periods, common usage still holds that they be typed with a period after each element and with no interior spacing. Use commas to set off these abbreviations when they follow a name, and eliminate the use of a courtesy title. (Mr., Mrs., Miss, Ms.) The title Dr. should not be used when it repeats the information given in the degree. Titles that do not repeat information may be used.

> Sara Tucker, M.D., will address the committee. ... **or** Dr. Sara Tucker will...
> Professor Diane Lewis, Ph.D., is preparing a lecture for the students.
> Vice-President Stephen R. Levine, J.D.

Here are just a few of the many academic degrees and religious orders and their abbreviations.

Bachelor of Arts	B.A.	Bachelor of Laws	LL.B.
Bachelor of Science	B.S.	Certified Public Accountant	C.P.A.
Master of Arts	M.A.	Doctor of Dental Surgery	D.D.S.

Medical Doctor	M.D.	Master of Business Administration	M.B.A.
Registered Nurse	R.N.	Society of Jesus	S.J.
Doctor of Divinity	D.D.	Doctor of Veterinary Medicine	D.V.M.
Doctor of Philosophy	Ph.D.	Bachelor of Fine Arts	B.F.A.
Juris Doctor	J.D.	Pharmaceutical Chemist	Ph.C.

Professional Designations.   The abbreviation *Esq.* for *Esquire* may be used by lawyers of either sex in place of the title *Attorney at Law.* Follow the lawyer's preference when known. A courtesy title is not used with either *Esq.* or *Attorney at Law.*

> Lorraine A. Murphy, Esq., is an associate at Barnes, Barnes & Wallace.

Organization and Company Names.   In writing a company or organization name, follow the company's preference for using abbreviations of such words as

Company	Co.	Limited	Ltd.
Corporation	Corp.	Manufacturers	Mfrs.
Incorporated	Inc.	Manufacturing	Mfg.
Brothers	Bros.		

The current trend is toward omitting commas around *Limited* or *Ltd.* and *Incorporated* or *Inc.,* but always follow company preferences.

Many companies and other organizations are referred to by their initials. Spell out the company name the first time it is used, followed by the abbreviation in parentheses. Type all such abbreviations in caps without periods or spaces.

AMA	YWCA	IBM	AT&T	SEC	NAACP
NBC	HMO	AFL-CIO	ABC	WPIX	UN

> A spokesman for the American Medical Association (AMA) discussed the dangers of secondhand smoke. Later in the conference AMA officials answered questions from the audience.

Acronyms.   An acronym is a word that has been coined from the initial letters of the words that make up the full name. For example, NATO is made up of the first letters of the North Atlantic Treaty Organization. Acronyms are written in all capitals and without punctuation. They are pronounced as words (ZIP or SALT) rather than letter by letter, as in the abbreviation YMCA. Since acronyms have been purposely coined to replace the longer terms they represent, they are appropriate for use in all but the most formal writing.

UNESCO	United Nations Educational, Scientific and Cultural Organization
BASIC	Beginner's All-purpose Symbolic Instruction Code
ZIP	Zone Improvement Plan
SALT	Strategic Arms Limitation Plan
OPEC	Organization of Petroleum Exporting Countries

Some acronyms are so commonly used that they have become words in their own right and no longer require capitalization.

laser	scuba	sonar	radar

Geographical Terms

Names of countries and national or geographic groupings are usually spelled out in text. If the repetition of such names is too time- and space-consuming, you may use an abbreviation once the full name has been given.

U.S.A.   U.K.   N.A.   B.W.I.

The names of states, territories, and possessions of the United States should be spelled out except in addresses and in tables. In tables use the abbreviations in the left column below. In an envelope address, use the approved ZIP Code abbreviation in the right column below.

Standard State Abbreviations

Ala.	Alas.	Ariz.
Ark.	Calif.	Colo.
Conn.	Del.	D.C.
Fla.	Ga.	Guam
Hawaii	Id.	Ill.
Ind.	Iowa	Kans.
Ky.	La.	Maine
Md.	Mass.	Mich.
Minn.	Miss.	Mo.
Mont.	Nebr.	Nev.
N.H.	N.J.	N.Mex.
N.Y.	N.C.	N.Dak.
Ohio	Okla.	Oreg.
Pa.	P.R.	R.I.
S.C.	S.Dak.	Tenn.
Tex.	Utah	Vt.
Va.	V.I.	Wash.
W.Va.	Wis.	Wyo.

ZIP Code Abbreviations

AL	AK	AZ	AR	CA
CO	CT	DE	DC	FL
GA	GU	HI	ID	IL
IN	IA	KS	KY	LA
ME	MD	MA	MI	MN
MS	MO	MT	NE	NV
NH	NJ	NM	NY	NC
ND	OH	OK	OR	PA
PR	RI	SC	SD	TN
TX	UT	VT	VA	VI
WA	WV	WI	WY	

NOTE: Some of the states, territories, and possessions shown above have no abbreviations except for ZIP Code abbreviations.

The word *Saint* in geographical names is often but not always abbreviated. Check a dictionary or atlas when in doubt. The abbreviation Ste. is derived from *Sainte,* a French word in the feminine gender meaning Saint.

St. Louis   St. Petersburg   St. Paul   Sault Ste. Marie

Spell out *Mount, Point, Fort,* and *Port* except in lists and tables.

Port Jervis   Mount Vernon   Fort Wayne   Point Lookout

The following words commonly used in **addresses** may be abbreviated in lists and tables but should be spelled out in running copy and in inside addresses and envelope addresses.

Avenue	Ave.	Boulevard	Blvd.	Square	Sq.
Place	Pl.	Drive	Dr.	Building	Bldg.
Road	Rd.	Lane	La.	Court	Ct.
Street	St.				

Compass Directions. Spell out compass directions except in the following special cases:

> When referring to the actual points of the compass or a directional bearing, use capital letters with no spaces or periods.

> N   S   E   W   SW   NE   NNW   SSE

> Her instructions are to fly compass bearing WSW from Pierre, South Dakota.

> When indicating a quadrant or section of a town or city in an address, the quadrant abbreviation is typed in full caps after the street name with no periods or spaces.

> 45 State Street NW

> The words latitude and longitude are always spelled out in copy.

> the polar latitudes   longitude 90 degrees west

Time and Time Zones. The abbreviations AM and PM are often used with numbers to express time. Most dictionaries show AM and PM as the first choice for these abbreviations, but A.M. and a.m., P.M. and p.m. are also considered acceptable. Never use these abbreviations with the redundant "in the morning," " in the evening," " noon," " at night," " in the afternoon," or "o'clock."

> 8 AM   9 in the morning   11 o'clock   10 PM

Time zones, when abbreviated, are typed all in caps without periods or spaces. (Some stylists still use periods.)

Eastern Standard Time	EST	Eastern Daylight Time	EDT
Central Standard Time	CST	Central Daylight Time	CDT
Pacific Standard Time	PST	Pacific Daylight Time	PDT
Mountain Standard Time	MST	Mountain Daylight Time	MDT

The names of days and weeks are always spelled out in running copy but may be abbreviated in lists.

Days of the Week			**Months of the Year**			
Sun.	Mon.		Jan.	Feb.	Mar.	Apr.
Tues.	Wed.		May	June	July	Aug.
Thurs.	Fri.	Sat.	Sep.	Oct.	Nov.	Dec.

The following, even shorter, abbreviations are used in indexes of periodic literature or sometimes in catalogs.

Su	M		Ja	F	Mr	Ap
Tu	W		My	Je	Jl	Au
Th	F	Sa	S	O	N	D

Always use the abbreviations A.D. (anno Domini) and B.C. (before Christ).

> A.D. 1990   384 B.C.

Other Abbreviations

Latin Abbreviations.   The trend for many years has been away from the use of Latin abbreviations entirely. Even the most commonly known such as

i.e. (*id est*) that is   e.g. (*exempli gratia*) for example
c. or ca. (*circa*) approximately   etc. (*et cetera*) and so forth

are better expressed by using their English equivalents. When using *etc.* or *and so forth,* be sure that the unknown elements of the series are known to the reader.

The child recited her alphabet: A, B, C, D, and so forth.

Symbols.   Use a dollar sign ($) with all but indefinite amounts of money and at the beginning of a sentence.

She owes me $45.
Nearly $10,000 was raised by the students.
The company lost several million dollars on that venture.
Ten thousand dollars is the price of the property.

Use an ampersand (&) only when it is part of the official title of a company or publication.

AT&T   ITT

Do not use a comma before an ampersand or the words *and Company.*

Other symbols (%, #, @, =, x, °) may be found on business forms and in technical material but should not be used in ordinary business communication.

Weights and Measures.   Units of measure are often abbreviated in technical material or in tables as follows:

inch(es)   in   millimeter(s)   mm
foot (feet) ft   centimeter(s)   cm
yard(s)   yd   kiloliter(s)   kl

NOTE: The abbreviation *in.* for *inch* and *inches* may retain its period to avoid confusion with *in,* which is a preposition.

Shortened Words.   Some words have shortened forms that are not abbreviations or acronyms. They are not capped nor are they followed by periods.

memo   lab   co-op   info   phone   exam

Chemical Elements.   The symbols for the chemical elements are one-, two-, or three-letter abbreviations of their official or Latin names. The abbreviations sometimes are used in text and always used in equations, formulas, and tables. No period follows the abbreviation.

aluminum   Al   neon   Ne   arsenic   As
plutonium Pu   carbon   C   zinc   Zn

Quick Study

In general, abbreviations are not used in typical business writing. You will, however, use the following on a regular basis:

Names: Initials when a person prefers them, Jr. and Sr.

Mr. J. R. Emming, Jr.

Courtesy and other titles: Mr., Mrs., Ms., Miss, Messrs., Mmes., Mss., Misses Dr., Esq.

Mr. and Mrs. Jonathan Taylor

Academic Degrees: B.A., Ph.D., M.D., D.D.S, and so forth

Angela Baskin, Ph. D.

Organization and company names when that is the preference of the company:

Co.	Inc.	AT&T	NAACP	UN

Time: 7 AM   9 PM

Symbols: $ for specific sums of money   & only when part of a company name

$50 $45.98   A & E Repair Shop

Addresses: Quadrant abbreviations where commonly used

Zip Code abbreviations for states

1500 Lincoln Avenue, NW
Washington, DC 20011

CHAPTER 2 # Sentence Structure

CHAPTER 2 # Sentence Structure

Sentence Structure

Using proper grammar is essential to communicating clearly and effectively. Learning the eight parts of speech, how sentences are constructed, and the different kinds of sentences will help you master the rules of grammar and write more effectively.

Parts of Speech

Every word in a sentence has a function. When you identify exactly what job a word does, the word can be classified as a particular part of speech. Remember that the job that a word does in a particular sentence, not the word itself, determines its part of speech. In any given sentence a word can have <u>only one job</u>, but a given word may perform different jobs in different sentences. This is why the dictionary often classifies a word as representing several different parts of speech.

The English language has eight parts of speech:

Noun	**Adjective**	**Conjunction**	**Verb**
Pronoun	**Adverb**	**Preposition**	**Interjection**

The **VERB** is the single most important word in a sentence. You cannot have a sentence without a verb, but you <u>can</u> have a sentence that consists of <u>only</u> a verb.

Stop!

<u>is</u> a sentence. It consists of only one word, and that one word is a verb.

The man in the bright yellow rain slicker by the side of the road

is <u>not</u> a sentence because it doesn't have a verb.

There are two kinds of verbs: linking verbs and action verbs

Linking Verbs express a condition or state of being. All forms of the verb *to be* are linking verbs:

am	are	is	was	were	be	been	being

Some other common linking verbs are

appear	seem	become	stay	remain	grow
hear	look	feel	taste	smell	sound

A linking verb is called linking because it must have a <u>complement</u> to complete the meaning begun by the subject and the verb.

The subject-verb combination *Mary is* makes no sense on its own.

The complement of a linking verb will be a noun or pronoun (predicate nominative) or an adjective (predicate adjective).

The predicate nominative provides another name for the subject.

Mary is a **teacher**.

The predicate adjective describes the subject.

Mary is **tall**.

Action Verbs express mental or physical action. They often have an object.

want	hope	need	desire	love
walk	run	sing	lift	cook

Action verbs do not necessarily require an object.

They <u>have been practicing.</u>   We <u>were reading.</u>

Many action verb sentences do, however, include an object, which will always be a noun or a noun equivalent.

Mary has a new **car**.
Mr. Hughes enjoys **playing golf**.
Laurence took the **report** home.

For the several kinds of objects, see below.

Some verbs can be linking verbs in one sentence and action verbs in another. If you can substitute *is* , *are* , *was*, or *were* for the verb, it's a linking verb. If you cannot, it's an action verb.

The bread *tastes* good.\= The bread *is* good. = <u>Linking verb</u>
They *tasted* the soup. = They *were* the soup. = <u>Action verb</u>

A **NOUN** names a person, place, thing, or idea. Nouns always answer the questions What? or Who? or Whom?

Nouns can be used as the subject, the direct object of a verb, the indirect object of a verb, or object of a preposition.

Subject:	The **mailman** always comes at 3 PM. (Tells *who* or *what* does or is something.)
Direct object:	I finally sold my **house**. (Tells *what* is sold.)
Indirect object:	Harry gave **Janet** a call. (Tells *to whom* he gave the call.)
Object of preposition:	She gave directions over the **telephone**. (Tells *what* is the object of the preposition *over*.)

PRONOUNS are used in place of a noun or another pronoun to avoid constant repetition of the same word. The noun or pronoun being replaced is called the <u>antecedent.</u>
Mary gave the book to Mary's brother.

Personal pronouns:	<u>She</u> gave <u>it</u> to <u>him.</u>
Indefinite pronouns:	<u>Someone</u> gave <u>something</u> to <u>somebody.</u>
Interrogative pronouns:	<u>Who</u> gave <u>what</u> to <u>whom?</u>

ADJECTIVES describe or modify nouns and pronouns. They answer the questions How many or much? Which one? What kind?

How many?	He bought <u>20</u> books.
Which one?	Bring me <u>that</u> poster.
What kind?	She bought a <u>red</u> dress.

ADVERBS describe or modify verbs, verbals, adjectives, and other adverbs. They answer the questions When? Where? How? To what extent? Phrases and clauses used as adverbs also answer the questions Under what circumstances? and Why?

When?	I'll see you <u>tomorrow.</u>
Where?	I'll see you <u>there.</u>
How?	She speaks <u>distinctly.</u>
To what extent?	See speaks <u>very</u> seriously.
Under what circumstances?	I will meet you <u>if I have the time.</u>
Why?	I did it <u>to please you.</u>

CONJUNCTIONS are used to connect words, phrases, and clauses.

Coordinate conjunctions are used to join two or more words, phrases, or clauses <u>of the same kind.</u> The eight coordinate conjunctions are *and, or, but, nor, either...or, neither...nor, both...and, not only...but also.*

Nouns:	*Both* <u>Mary</u> *and* <u>John</u> are going to the movies.
Verbs:	Mary <u>dances</u> *but* <u>does</u> not <u>sing</u> in the play.
Prepositional Phrases:	He jogs *either* <u>before breakfast</u> *or* <u>after lunch.</u>
Adjective Clauses:	He needs an assistant <u>who is enthusiastic</u> *and* <u>who is willing to learn.</u>
Infinitives:	He likes <u>to fish</u> and <u>to swim.</u>

Subordinate (dependent) conjunctions join dependent clauses to independent clauses and show the relationship that exists between the two.

I went to the store *because* <u>I needed staples.</u>
<u>*If*</u> <u>he calls,</u> tell him I am not in.
I wonder *whether* <u>he got the book I sent.</u>

A **PREPOSITION** is a word that shows the relationship between its object and some other word in the sentence.

> Put the box *under* the table.
> Put the box *on* the table.
> Put the box *near* the table.

In the above sentences *table* is the object of the preposition. The prepositions *under*, *on*, and *near* show the relationships between the box and the table. The preposition + its object + any words that modify the object are called a prepositional phrase.

Prepositional phrases can function as nouns, adjectives, or adverbs.

An **INTERJECTION** is a word that expresses strong feeling. It is followed by an exclamation point or a comma because it has no grammatical connection to the rest of the sentence.

> Well, try a different approach.
> Help! We can't balance our books until we get your check.

Verbals

Closely related to the parts of speech are the three verbals: *gerunds, participles*, and *infinitives*. A verbal comes from a verb, looks like a verb, but functions as another part of speech.

Type	Form	Function	Examples
gerund	verb + ing	noun	swimming, running
participle	verb + ed or en or ing	adjective	washed, written, speaking
infinitive	to + verb	noun adjective adverb	to run, to walk

> **Gerund:** Swimming is my favorite sport.
> **Participle:** The swimming pool is not heated.
> **Infinitive:** We want to swim in the pool.

A verbal + its subject and/or complement + any modifiers is called a **verbal phrase**.

> **Gerund phrase:** Swimming in the ocean is my favorite sport
> **Participial phrase:** The train leaving from Track 4 is late.
> **Infinitive phrase:** He wanted me to see that new movie.

Phrases

A phrase is a group of words that

> does not have a subject-verb combination
> cannot stand alone to express a complete thought
> acts as a single part of speech—verb, adjective, adverb, or noun

Clauses

A clause is a group of words that has a subject and a verb. A clause may be classified as independent or dependent.

An **independent clause** is a group of words that

> has a subject-verb combination
> can stand alone to express a complete thought
> may be joined to another clause, dependent or independent.

Independent clause
She will proofread the report

Dependent clause
while I file the folders in the drawer.

A **dependent clause** is a group of words that

> has a subject-verb combination
> cannot stand alone to express a complete thought
> acts as a single part of speech—adjective, adverb, or noun.

To determine whether a clause is dependent or independent, read every word in the clause as one unit; then decide whether that unit expresses a complete thought.

NOTE: When the first word of the clause is *because, that, who, if, while,* and so forth, the clause is dependent. (See subordinate conjunctions, page 37.)

A **sentence** is a group of words that

> has at least one subject-verb combination
> stands alone to express a complete thought
> begins with a capital letter and concludes with end punctuation

Every sentence has two basic parts—the subject and the predicate.

The subject consists of the noun; pronoun; or word, phrase, or clause used as a noun that performs the action of the verb or is being talked about in the sentence. You can find the subject by asking Who? or What? of the verb. The complete subject also includes any words, phrases, or clauses that describe or modify the subject.

The predicate is the verb that is saying something about the subject. The complete predicate also includes any complements, objects, and words, phrases, or clauses that describe or modify the verb.

Complete subject
The tall man in the back of the room

Complete predicate
gave me a copy of the program.

Never separate with a single mark of punctuation a subject from its verb or a verb from its complement or object.

Examine the following sentences, which illustrate the use of words, phrases, and clauses.

| **Nouns** | John likes what? |
| | |

	Noun:	John likes tennis.
	Infinitive phrase:	John likes to play tennis.
	Gerund phrase:	John likes playing tennis.
	Noun clause:	John likes what he does for a living.

Adjectives   Which woman is my employer?

	Adjective:	That woman is my employer.
	Prepositional phrase:	The woman in the back is my employer.
	Infinitive phrase:	The woman to ask is my employer.
	Participial phrase:	The woman sitting in the back is my employer.
	Adjective clause:	The woman who is in the back is my employer.

Adverbs   When and why does he run?

	Adverb:	He runs early.
	Prepositional phrase:	He runs in the morning.
	Infinitive phrase:	He runs to keep fit.
	Adverbial clause:	He runs when the sun is rising.

Sentences Classified by Structure

Sentences are classified according to structure as *simple, compound, complex,* or *compound-complex.*

A **simple sentence** has one subject and one verb, either or both of which may be compound.

> Joe is checking the invitations.
> Joe and Pat are checking the invitations. (COMPOUND SUBJECT)
> Joe is checking and mailing the invitations. (COMPOUND VERB)
> Joe checked the invitations and then mailed them. (COMPOUND VERB)
> Joe and Pat are checking and mailing the invitations. (COMPOUND SUBJECT AND COMPOUND VERB)

A **compound sentence** has at least two independent clauses. Therefore, a compound sentence always has at least two subject-verb combinations.

> Joe is checking the invitations, and Pat is mailing them.

For punctuation of compound sentences, see page 47.

A **complex sentence** has one independent clause and one or more dependent clauses.

> Roger will file those papers after I have checked them.
> Roger will file those papers = INDEPENDENT CLAUSE
> after I have checked them = DEPENDENT CLAUSE

John is the man who called yesterday.
John is the man = INDEPENDENT CLAUSE
who called yesterday = DEPENDENT CLAUSE

A **compound-complex sentence** has at least two independent clauses and at least one dependent clause.

Your résumé indicates excellent qualifications, and we would like to arrange an interview time when we call you on Monday.

Your résumé indicates excellent qualifications = INDEPENDENT CLAUSE
we would like to arrange an interview time = INDEPENDENT CLAUSE
when we call you on Monday = DEPENDENT CLAUSE

An **elliptical sentence** is one in which one or more words have intentionally been omitted that the reader can fill in easily and naturally. The fact that a sentence is elliptical does not affect the classification of the sentence by structure or purpose.

An elliptical adverbial clause is frequently introduced by *than* or *as*.

She did more work on the project *than I.* (than I did)
We are as eager to complete the project *as you.* (as you are)

In imperative sentences *you* is usually the implied subject.

(You) Read that file before you proceed.
(You) Give a copy of the memo to Barbara.

Additional examples of elliptical sentences:

Kathy completed the filing; Maureen, the correspondence.
(Maureen completed the correspondence.)

While there, he met with Senator Burns.
(While he was there)

Had you been here, you would have met the President.
(If you had been here)

This morning I interviewed three applicants; this afternoon, two.
(This afternoon I interviewed two applicants.)

Sentences Classified by Purpose

Sentences are classified according to the writer's purpose and are punctuated based on those classifications.

Declarative: states a fact or something represented as fact.

She will type while I file.
I wonder whether they have arrived.

Imperative: makes a request or gives a command. (The subject of an imperative sentence is usually implied.)

> (You) Close the door. (gives a command)
> (You) Please return the enclosed card. (makes a request)

Interrogative: asks a question.

> Did you finish the book?

Exclamatory: expresses strong feeling. (Exclamatory sentences are seldom used in business writing except in advertising and sales.)

> You may have already won $50,000!

CHAPTER 3 **Punctuation**

CHAPTER 3 **Punctuation**

Punctuation

Punctuation is used to make written language more readable. Proper punctuation depends entirely on the functions of words, phrases, and clauses and the structure of the sentence.

Internal Punctuation

Punctuation is used within a sentence for four reasons:

1. To separate
2. To introduce
3. To set off nonessential constructions
4. To emphasize

Punctuation to Separate

Series. A series consists of three or more words, phrases, or clauses that are grammatically the same.

Use commas to separate the members of a series unless all the items are joined by *and* or *or*. A comma is placed after each member of the series except the last.

Meetings will be held on **Monday, Tuesday,** *and* **Wednesday.** (NOUNS)

Write, telephone, *or* **visit** your dealer today. (VERBS)

We looked **in the file, on the desk,** *and* **behind the bookcase.**
(PREPOSITIONAL PHRASES)

The booklet tells you **what to take with you, what to leave at home,** *and* **how to handle foreign currency.** (INFINITIVE PHRASES)

The arbitrator tries to settle differences **quietly, quickly, fairly.** (ADVERBS)

In a year's time her newspaper column has covered **politics and penology, finance and foreign policy, diplomacy and deficit spending.** (NOUNS IN PAIRS)

The design is available **in gold** *and* **in silver** *and* **in platinum.**
(PREPOSITIONAL PHRASES)

I will meet you on **Monday** *or* **Tuesday** *or* **Wednesday.** (NOUNS)

A series of independent clauses is treated like any other series.

Sign your name at the bottom of the contract, put it in the envelope, and mail it to me as soon as possible.

For a series in a company name, always follow the preference of the firm.

Richardson Roberts Wingate & Smith   Peat, Marwick, Mitchell & Co.

NOTE: Many editors consider the comma before the conjunction optional if omitting it does not cause misreading. <u>In business writing, however, the comma is required.</u>

Use a semicolon to separate the members of a series with internal punctuation.

> Meetings will be held on **Monday, June 4; Tuesday, June 5;** *and* **Friday, June 8.**

> We will hear reports from **James White, business manager; Lisa Blaine, director of marketing;** *and* **Richard Thomas, comptroller.**

> We have branch offices in **Lincoln, Nebraska; Chicago, Illinois;** *and* **Wilmington, Delaware.**

> The chairman reported **that the company now produces plastics, alloys, and textile fibers; that it serves industry, agriculture, and the government;** *and* **that one of its greatest needs is people with inquiring minds.**

Compound Sentences. An <u>independent clause</u> has a subject and a verb and is able to stand alone as a complete thought.

A <u>compound sentence</u> contains two or more independent clauses.

The independent clauses in a compound sentence are frequently joined to one another by conjunctions:

and	either . . .or
or	neither . . .nor
but	both. . . and
nor	not only. . . but also

Use a comma before the conjunction to separate the independent clauses in a compound sentence.

> He typed the report, *and* she brought it to the printer's office.
> (You) Open up the mail at once, *and* (you) give it to Mrs. Jones.

> *Not only* was the report sloppily edited, *but* it was *also* factually incorrect.

If either of the independent clauses contains fewer than four words, the comma is optional.

> He signed the card (,) *and* I mailed it.

NOTE: In a sentence beginning with *please, please* is the verb. Do <u>not</u> put a comma between the two verbals *sign* and *mail* in the following example:

> (You) Please sign the enclosed card and mail it today.

Use a semicolon to separate two independent clauses that are not joined by a conjunction.

> We ordered the equipment last week; it has yet to be delivered.
> We ordered the equipment last week; however, it has yet to be delivered.

Use a semicolon to separate two independent clauses when either contains internal punctuation.

> We ordered the equipment on Tuesday, May 3; *but* it has not yet been delivered.

> They planned the project for Monday, Tuesday, and Wednesday; *but* they completed it on Tuesday.

Some compound sentences are elliptical, which means the verb has been omitted but is clearly understood in the second or following independent clauses. Other words may also be omitted in this way. Punctuate the compound sentence according to the above rules, and put a comma where the verb is missing.

> Our Albany plant hired 11 new employees, *and* our Washingtonville plant, 15. (Washingtonville plant hired 15.)

> Huntington needs four more copies of the textbook; Providence, three; New York, seven; *and* Boston, one. (Providence needs three copies; New York needs seven copies; and Boston needs one copy.)

Degree-result clauses. Use a comma to separate degree-result clauses. Elliptical clauses of this type are often quite short and need no punctuation.

> The sooner we get your check in the mail, the sooner you can start enjoying *Newsweek*.

> The sooner the better.   The more the merrier.

Absolute Phrases. An <u>absolute phrase</u> is an infinitive or participial phrase that has its own subject. It adds information to the sentence but is not *structurally* related to the sentence.

Use a comma to separate an absolute phrase from the rest of the sentence.

> **Weather permitting**, the company picnic will be held on the 9th.
> The new manual will cost $10,000, **our obligation to pay half.**

Adjectives Before the Noun. <u>Coordinate adjectives</u> modify the noun separately and equally. They can be read smoothly with the word *and* inserted between them or can be reversed without affecting the meaning of the sentence.

<u>Noncoordinate adjectives</u> cannot be reversed without changing the meaning of the sentence nor can *and* be smoothly inserted between them.

Use a comma to separate two coordinate adjectives. Never put a comma between an adjective and its noun, between noncoordinate adjectives, or between a coordinate and a noncoordinate adjective.

> **Coordinate:**   **New, innovative remedial** programs are being planned.
> (*and* can be inserted between *new* and *innovative*)

> **Noncoordinate:**   We will need to fill out **several extra withholding tax** forms.
> (*and* cannot be inserted between any of the four adjectives)

NOTE: When you are puzzling over whether to use a comma between adjectives, try reading the sentence to yourself with the word *and*. If the sentence makes good sense that way, insert a comma instead of *and*.

Addresses.   Use commas to separate the items in an address when it appears in a sentence.

> They moved to 90 Locust Street, Savannah, Georgia, soon after his birth.

Numbers.   Use commas to make numbers more readable by separating them.
Between two figures.

> On March **21, 87** persons attended the seminar.
> The conference has been scheduled for January **17, 1996.**

Between two words.

> Of the **nine, six** were present.

In numbers with five or more digits. (Four-digit numbers may take a comma. Follow company style.)

> The bill came to **$19,325.98.**

Time, Initials, Subtitles, Footnotes, Plays.   Use a colon to separate the hour from the minutes in expressions of time.

> **11:30** AM   **4:45** in the morning

Use a colon to separate the dictator's from the transcriber's initials.

> **JFT:KH**   **LH:VF**   **IMS:jt**

Use a colon to separate a book title and subtitle.

> **Thomas Jefferson: Private Letters**

Use a colon to separate the act and scene of a play.

> **Act II:3**

For Clarity.   Use a comma to separate two words that might be misread.

> To George, Washington was a beautiful city.
> Whatever is, is right.
> Soon after, the board voted to issue the new stock.

Punctuation to Introduce

An introductory word, phrase, or dependent clause precedes the subject of the clause it modifies. It sometimes modifies a word in that clause; it sometimes serves to introduce the entire clause.

Introductory Clauses.   A <u>dependent clause</u> is a group of words with a subject and a verb that functions as one part of speech (an adjective, an adverb, or a noun) and does not stand alone to make a complete thought.

Place a comma after any introductory dependent clause.

> **While Mr. Clark was in Washington,** he addressed the Press Club. (ADVERBIAL CLAUSE) (verb *was*; subordinate conjunction is *while*)
>
> We have agreed upon the terms of the contract, and **if signatures are obtained this week,** work can begin on April 1. (ADVERBIAL CLAUSE)
>
> **If after you have read the manual, you would like to have a salesman call,** please telephone this office. (TWO INTRODUCTORY ADVERBIAL CLAUSES)
>
> **That the market will rise soon,** he firmly believes. (NOUN CLAUSE)

An introductory clause can be elliptical—that is, one or more words are unstated but clearly implied. The punctuation remains the same.

> **While there,** he interviewed several applicants. (*While* **he was** there,...)
> **Should you be detained,** please call me. (**If** you should be detained,...)
> **If you are available,** call me; **if not,** we'll make another date. (If **you are** not.)

No comma follows the introductory clause when it is preceded by an adverb and the word order in the main clause is inverted.

> **Only when you experience our services** will you see why more people choose American Airlines. (NO PUNCTUATION)

Introductory Phrases.   A <u>phrase</u> is a group of words that functions as one part of speech (an adjective, an adverb, or a noun). A phrase may contain a verb or a verbal but cannot stand alone to make a complete thought.

Use a comma after an introductory phrase that contains a verb or verbal. (Look for the verb form.) The length of the phrase makes no difference.

Introductory Participial Phrases:

Having been elected, Mrs. Jones expressed her appreciation to the members.

Mr. Hudson said that **based on last month's earnings,** the figures indicate an encouraging trend.

Introductory Infinitive Phrases:

To qualify, one must be a high school graduate.
In order to better prepare for the test, she took an SAT review course.
To transcribe the minutes accurately, the secretary must take careful notes.

Introductory Prepositional Phrases: (Occasionally one of these phrases may appear without its preposition.)

Before signing, read the contract carefully.
From what she told us, the location is excellent.
The day she was here, we discussed the proposal. (**On** the day she was here.)

Even without a verb form, an introductory phrase of five or more words is followed by a comma.

> **Because of certain major design changes,** we expect better mileage in our new model car.
>
> **In addition to her responsibilities in the Accounting Department,** she often fills in for the personnel manager.

The current trend is toward omitting the comma after a short phrase that does not contain a verb or verbal.

> **In the fall** she will enter Harvard.
> **On Friday** we have our regular staff meeting.
> **For thirty years** he has worked for the same company.

Omit the comma after an introductory phrase if the word order in the main clause is inverted.

> **In a newspaper article last week** appeared a reference to our company.
> (NO PUNCTUATION)

Position is a very important factor in determining proper punctuation. The introductory clauses and phrases illustrated above, when placed elsewhere in the sentence, would **not** be punctuated.

> He firmly believes **that the market will rise soon.**
> Work can begin on April 1 **if signatures are obtained this week.**
> She took an SAT review course **in order to prepare for the test.**
> Read the contract carefully **before signing.**

Introductory Transitional Expressions. A transitional expression is a word or phrase that shows the relationship between a preceding and a following idea. Here are a few examples:

above all	finally	in fact	of course
as a result	for instance	in other words	on the whole
at any rate	fortunately	in summary	therefore
by the way	however	moreover	typically
consequently	in addition	obviously	unfortunately

Use a comma after an introductory transitional expression.

> **Above all,** we are interested in the quality of our product.
> Our workers are fixing the lines; **therefore,** service should be restored soon.
>
> **Finally,** we have updated our listings, and **as a result,** we can give you the most up-to-date information.

The following short conjunctive adverbs are normally not followed by a comma: **also, hence, then, still, yet.**

> Our plant has been operating 24 hours a day; **yet** we have been unable to fill all the orders.

Introductory Adverbs.   An introductory adverb or short prepositional phrase used as an adverb (most answer the question When?) should not be followed by a comma.

The following are typical:

at present	in the future	previously
at the same time	meanwhile	probably
for some time	occasionally	some time ago
for that reason	often	under the circumstances
generally	perhaps	usually

Instead we request that you fill out Order Form 294.
In the meantime we shall credit your account.
Under the circumstances we shall return your merchandise by next month.

Introductory Words.   Use a comma after one or more **introductory adjectives** that precede an article *(a, an, the)*, a pronoun, or a proper noun.

Tired and frustrated, the picketers finally gave up.
Always ambitious, he will certainly succeed.
Dignified and diplomatic, Mr. Law is my first choice.

Use a comma after a short **admonition** when the connective **that** is unexpressed.

Remember, the customer is always right.
Don't forget, this cutback will have far-reaching consequences.
Just think, we have almost reached our goal!

but. . .

Remember that the customer is always right.
Don't forget that this cutback will have far-reaching consequences.
Just think that we have almost reached our goal.

Use a colon after the **salutation** to introduce the body of the letter.

Dear Mr. Dexter: Ladies: Dear Sir:

Use a colon after a **subject introduction.**

Subject: Stockholders' Meeting

Punctuation To Set Off Nonessential Constructions

A <u>nonessential element</u> is one that can be removed from the sentence without substantially changing its meaning. All nonessential elements are set off from the rest of the sentence, meaning the same mark of punctuation is used both before and after the nonessential element.

Check that you have punctuated properly by reading over the sentence, leaving out the nonessential part, to make sure the sentence still makes sense. Although the information in a nonessential element may be of importance to the reader (otherwise, why include it?), it is not needed to make a meaningful sentence.

Adjective Clauses.   An <u>adjective clause</u> is a dependent clause that is used as an adjective. It typically follows the noun that it describes. An adjective clause will begin with one of the following: *who, whom, whose* (to describe people), *which, that* (to describe things) or *when* or *where*. Note that these pronouns are sometimes preceded by a preposition.

An adjective clause, when not needed to specifically identify the noun it modifies, is nonessential and is set off with a comma or a pair of commas. If the noun it modifies is a proper noun; is already identified by a number, a letter, a date, an amount of money, or a specific time; has been previously mentioned; or is limited in some other way, the adjective clause is nonessential.

If the adjective clause is the <u>only</u> identification of the noun, it is essential and not punctuated.

Nonessential:

Mr. John Haven , *whom you have just met,* is our corporate counsel.

(*Mr. John Haven* is a proper noun.) *Mr. John Haven is our corporate counsel* makes sense without the adjective clause.

Essential:

The man *whom you have just met* is our corporate counsel.

(*Man* is a common noun. *The man is our corporate counsel* does not make sense without the adjective clause, because the reader does not know which man you are talking about.

Other examples:

Ms. Joan Hernandez, *who answers the phone in the outer office,* is my new secretary.

The young woman *who answered the phone* is my new secretary.

Mr. Wilson, *in whom I have great confidence,* is a young man with a future.

Mr. Wilson is a young man *in whom I have great confidence.*

Thank you for your check for $75, *which covers your June balance.*

Thank you for the check *that you recently sent our organization.*

The Texaco Company, *which has its headquarters in Dallas,* is growing at its fastest pace in 10 years.

Texaco is a company *that is growing at its fastest pace in 10 years.*

An essential adjective clause uses *that* as a connective; a nonessential one uses *which.* When a sentence already contains a clause beginning with *that,* however, use *which* for the adjective clause but don't punctuate it. You may also leave it out. In this case *that* is used rather that *which.*

We understand *that* the time *which* you indicated is only estimated.
We understand the time that you indicated is only estimated.

Adjective clauses beginning with the following and similar expressions are always nonessential and for that reason are set off with a comma or pair of commas.

a copy of which	several of which (whom)
all of whom (which)	some of which (whom)
each of which (whom)	reference to which (whom)
either of which (whom)	a few of which (whom)

Prices are given on page 71 of the catalog, **a copy of which** we sent you recently.

These employees, **several of whom** have degrees in engineering, did a fine job on this project.

Adverbial Clauses. Most adverbial clauses are essential to the meaning of the sentence and are not punctuated. Some, however, occur at the end of the sentence and merely add information not necessary to the understanding of the previous clause. Set off these clauses with a comma. Look for the following connectives:

although	particularly, perhaps, possibly,
as, for, or since (in place of because)	probably
despite the fact that	regardless of
especially	so or so that (meaning as a
even if, ... though	result, consequently, therefore)
however many,... much,... few	whatever
in spite of the fact that	whereas
no matter how,...when,...where	whether
now that	whether or not
only to (verb) that	whoever (meaning no matter who)

You will pay only $7.95, **although the retail price is $11.95.**

We are pleased to give you an extension, **especially since your order arrived several days late.**

I look forward to discussing this important issue with you, **possibly when you come to New York next month.**

Short Nonessential Clauses. Set off a short nonessential clause, one that interrupts the sentence pattern, with commas.

Mr. Lansing will, **we believe,** return on May 1.
American Electronics has, **as you know,** enlarged its old plant.
The advertising program, **Mrs. Burden says,** begins on June 15.
Mrs. Sherman, **when told of her promotion,** seemed surprised.

When a short independent clause follows the connective for an adjective clause, the independent clause is essential to the meaning of the sentence and is not punctuated.

Mr. Niven is the man *who* **I believe** *won the election.*

Nonessential Questions. Set off with a comma or commas a nonessential question used simply to confirm the statement. The sentence ends in a question mark.

Mr. Dennison is, **is he not,** the chairman of the board?
She has grown in her role of administrator, **has she not?**

Participial Phrases.   A <u>participial phrase</u> is a verbal phrase used as an adjective. It follows the same rules as adjective clauses—that is, it is set off with a comma or comma when not necessary to the identification of the noun it modifies.

> Mr. Ames, **addressing the meeting,** said that profits were improving.
> The man **addressing the meeting** is Mr. Ames.
> Thank you for your letter of September 10**, inviting us to next month's meeting.**
> Thank you for your letter **inviting us to next month's meeting.**

Words such as *concerning, regarding, pertaining to, referring to,* and *relating to* may at first look like participles but in fact are prepositions. Prepositional phrases beginning with these words are not punctuated.

> Thank you for your letter of March 7 **concerning our summer flights.**
> Mr. Tate's letter **regarding the changes in the schedule** will receive our immediate attention.

Parenthetic Elements.   <u>Parenthetic elements</u> either interrupt the flow of the main idea or add an idea to the end of the sentence. In either case, parenthetic elements are set off by commas.

Interrupting Phrases.   When a prepositional phrase beginning with one of the following expressions separates the subject from its verb, set off the phrase with commas.

accompanied by	as well as	in addition to	minus	together with
along with	besides	including	plus	yet not
and not	but not	instead of	rather than	

> Mr. Webb, **along with his two aides,** will leave for Chicago tomorrow.
> Was the furniture, **together with the carpeting,** delivered today?
> I asked them to deliver the furniture **together with the carpeting.**

Set off with commas a short interrupting phase ending with *after, before, or since.*

> We were familiar with the layout because, **a short time before,** we had inspected the premises.
> He took advantage of the trial offer and, **ever since,** has been a regular customer.

Set off with commas a prepositional phrase that breaks the continuity of the sentence thought.

> The dividend, **for the time being at least,** will remain at 75 cents a share.

Additional Prepositional Phrases.   Put a comma before a nonessential prepositional phrase beginning with one of the following words when it comes at the end of a sentence.

despite	in spite of	particularly	possibly	probably
especially	irrespective of	perhaps	preferably	regardless of

> The geologists will continue the survey, **regardless of the weather.**
> Please call me at the office, **preferably after three o'clock.**

Punctuation

Infinitive Phrases.   Set off with commas a nonessential infinitive phrase.

> The meeting, *to be sure*, was not as productive as it could have been.
> You did more than we expected, *to say the least.*

Independent and Transitional Expressions.   Independent and transitional expressions may be used in the middle or at the end of a clause. When they are used in this way, set them off with commas. See list on page 51.

> Mr. Byrnes, **on the other hand,** found several errors.
> No department, **furthermore,** will escape the reductions in the budget.
> There is, **no doubt,** a problem with the system.
> I, **too,** wonder about her effectiveness as a teacher.

Commas may be omitted around any of these expressions if you wish to use the expressions to give emphasis to the sentence instead of using them parenthetically.

> She will **of course** make every effort to attend the meeting.
> Mr. Jones is **therefore** very effective as a supervisor.

Appositives.   An <u>appositive</u> is a noun, usually with modifiers, that follows another noun or a pronoun and identifies, renames, or explains the first noun. An appositive can occasionally begin with *or* , *such as* , or *as*.

Set off with a comma or pair of commas a nonessential appositive—that is, one that is not needed to identify the noun it follows.

> I discussed the matter with Miss Clay, **my financial adviser.**
> The convention will convene on Monday, **August 6,** in Milwaukee.
> My financial advisor, **Miss Clay,** discussed next year's tax revisions.
> Jack Poole, **as project manager,** accepted the award.
> I have ordered all the filing supplies, **such as files, tabs, and labels.**
> Micrology, **or attention to petty details,** characterizes the mindset of far too many supervisors.
> The meeting will be held in Albany, **New York,** next month.

An appositive is essential when it is necessary to identify the noun or pronoun it follows. Do not punctuate an essential appositive. Note: These appositives often follow the pattern *the* + common noun + proper noun.

> My brother **Tom** gave the toast at the wedding.
> She quoted from the essay **"Self-Reliance"** by Emerson.
> The word **inconvenience** is frequently misspelled.
> The novelist **Anna Quindlan** spoke about her new novel.

Nonessential Adjectives.   Use commas to set off nonessential adjectives that follow the noun they modify.

> The speaker, **undismayed,** continued his presentation.
> Those trees, **young and old,** retard erosion.

Not all adjectives following the noun they modify are nonessential. If the meaning of the sentence would be altered without them, do not punctuate.

> We are seeking students **willing and able** to assume responsibility.

Direct address. Set off with a comma or commas a name or title used in direct address.

> **Mr. McNeil,** we hope you will accept the chairmanship.
> We understand, **gentlemen,** your reluctance to commit yourselves now.

Contrasting and Limiting Ideas. Set off with a comma or commas a contrasting idea beginning with *not, seldom,* or *never* or a limiting idea beginning with *but.* This rule does not apply to the correlative conjunction *not only...but also.*

> She ordered dark, **not light,** beer.
> *National Outlook* is available only by subscription, *never on newsstands.*
> The club will be open on Sunday, **but only for members.**
> The secretary represents **not only** his company **but also** his executive.

And so forth, inclusive, respectively, limited, and incorporated
Set off with a comma or commas the above-mentioned words.

> Pages 419 to 423, **inclusive,** were deleted, were they not?
> For the offices of governor and lieutenant governor, we nominated Mr. Crane and Ms. Archer, **respectively.**
> Williams and Williams, **Limited,** received the contract.
> Send the memo to each department: Accounting, Research, Personnel, Marketing, **and so forth.**
> Ogden and Gregory, **Incorporated,** has offices in this building.
>
> (Follow company style. Many companies do not set off *incorporated* in their company names.)

For the use of commas with academic degree abbreviations, names, Jr., Sr., and Esq., see Abbreviations page 27.

Punctuation For Emphasis

Many grammatical constructions that are set off with commas when in their simplest form, are set off with other, more dramatic punctuation when complicated with internal punctuation or when worded in such a way as to emphasize them. Although some of these constructions are used routinely in everyday business correspondence, others are seen most frequently in advertising or sales writing. All of them, in one way or another, are intended to draw attention to themselves.

Emphatic Appositives. When the wording of a sentence leads the reader to expect an explanation, use a colon or (even more emphatic) a dash to give emphasis to the explanation.

> Our department store has one policy: *The customer is always right.*
> Our goal is the same: *to satisfy our customers and our shareholders.*
> We prize one quality above all others—*integrity.*

Note the difference between an emphatic appositive and a nonemphatic appositive. A nonemphatic appositive would not be missed if omitted from the sentence. If you omit an emphatic appositive from the sentence, the reader may be left wondering.

Nonemphatic: I'd like you to meet my boss, **Mrs. Williams.**
(Leaving out the appositive doesn't leave the reader wanting more)

Emphatic: We prize one quality above all others—**integrity.**
(Leaving out the appositive would leave the reader saying What quality is above all others?)

Run-on Enumerations.   Use a colon after the introduction to a run-on enumeration. If the items are independent clauses, the first word after the colon is capitalized; otherwise, only a proper noun or adjective is capped.

Our company has two objectives: (1) We hope to give the public superior television, and (2) we hope to give shareholders superior profits.

You attest to these assertions when you endorse a check: (a) that the check is genuine and valid, (b) that you have received value for it, and (c) that you will pay for it yourself if necessary.

Tabulations.   Use a colon after the introduction to a tabulation. Capitalize the first word of each tabulated item.

Our secretaries' duties may be summed up under these headings:

1. Opening and blue-penciling mail
2. Answering the telephone and making appointments
3. Transcribing letters, memos, and reports
4. Taking minutes at meetings and conferences

Run-on enumerations and tabulations are more elaborate versions of the emphatic appositive. More attention is drawn to the run-on because of the lettering or numbering. Both the numbering and the effective use of white space make the tabulation stand out on a page.

Use a colon only after an introduction that is a complete sentence.

INCORRECT: The committee includes: Mr. Thompson, Miss Wilson, and. Ms. Smith.

CORRECT: The committee includes these members: Mr. Thompson, Miss Wilson, and Ms. Smith.

INCORRECT: Our secretaries' duties may be summed up under:
1. Opening and blue-penciling mail
2. Answering the telephone
3. Transcribing notes from handwritten copy.

CORRECT: Our secretaries' duties may be summed up under these headings:
1. Opening and blue-penciling mail
2. Answering the telephone
3. Transcribing notes from handwritten copy.

Summary Words.   Use a dash before a noun or pronoun that follows and summarizes a list of two or more words, phrases, or clauses. Though less usual, single words can also be used in this way.

> Enthusiasm and imagination—these are the qualities our employees must have.
>
> The Statue of Liberty, the World Trade Center, Battery Park—all are visible from the windows of his new office.
>
> Money—it's the root of all evil!

To show a sudden shift in thought.   Use dashes to set off a word, phrase, or clause that creates a sudden shift in the flow of the sentence thought.

> Can he—*indeed, should he*—attempt to acquire another company?
> She's a generous employer—*too generous!*

Punctuated Appositives.   Use a dash or dashes to set off an appositive that already contains punctuation. Such appositives may be introduced by *namely, for instance, for example,* and *that is.*

> Telephone calls to moving vehicles—**cars, trains, buses, and trucks**—may be made using your cellular phone.
>
> Our mobile service operator will be ready to assist you in calling any distant moving vehicle—**boats, planes, helicopters, or trains.**
>
> The office manager is in charge of ordering all office supplies—**for example, notebooks, paper, pens, and staplers.**
>
> A small piece of luggage—**for instance, a cosmetic case**—is all you may carry on to the plane.

You can also use a colon when the list is at the end of the sentence and does not begin with an introductory expression.

We must consider three important factors: **sales, profits, and expenses.**

Nonessential Adjectives.   Use dashes to set off a series of nonessential adjectives that follows the noun it modifies.

> Many businesses—**small, medium, and large**—can profit from our services.

Parentheses ( )

Parentheses usually enclose material related to the sentence thought but not to the sentence structure. Such material provides supplementary information or directions to the reader. Parentheses tend to de-emphasize the words enclosed.

Use parentheses to enclose **supplementary information** that is independent of the main sentence structure, often an independent clause.

> Mr. Robert's company **(Kenneco is the name it recently adopted)** is showing continued strong operating performance.

Use parentheses to enclose abbreviations, dates, and explanations that provide extra information.

> The American Booksellers Association (ABA) will hold its meeting Friday.
> The Bicentennial (1976) was a year-long celebration.
> Their source of information (the Internet) was their most important communications link.

Use parentheses to enclose editorial cross-references. References at the end of a sentence may be considered part of the main sentence or as a separate sentence.

> Costs rose in 1995 (figure 10).
> Remember, verbals are not verbs. (See page 92.)

Use parentheses to enclose numbers or letters used in a run-on enumeration or in an outline.

Capitalization with Parentheses.   Within a sentence the first word of the enclosed material is capitalized only if it is a proper noun, a proper adjective, or the pronoun *I.*

> We understand that its overseas growth (we have just learned of the new plant in Milan) has been spectacular.

When the parenthetic material is not part of another sentence, capitalize the first word and use the appropriate end punctuation.

> The annual meeting was held in Memphis. (A copy of the program is enclosed.)

Parentheses with Other Punctuation.   Do not use a period after a declarative statement enclosed in parentheses. Do use an exclamation point or question mark when appropriate. Such marks go before the closing parenthesis.

> Our latest publication (thank you for your help with the research) will be in bookstores by July.

> The landscaping of Bloomfield Hills Park (you were the designer, weren't you?) is receiving national acclaim.

A question mark enclosed in parentheses expresses doubt about the information that precedes it.

> The two companies merged in 1994 *(?)* and moved to New Jersey.

Within a sentence never place a punctuation mark before the opening parenthesis. Place any punctuation required at that point after the closing parenthesis.

> If we should decide to send an exhibit (we are not certain yet), we will call you. (COMMA FOR THE INTRODUCTORY CLAUSE)

Brackets [ ]

Brackets are always used in pairs.

Use brackets to enclose **additions, corrections, or explanations inserted in quoted material.** (A writer uses parentheses to add information; an editor uses brackets.)

> Our Cleveland distributor writes: "Our stock is down to three dozen sets of UHF strips [he means VHF], and we must have another shipment at once."

Use brackets to set off the Latin word *sic,* meaning "*thus,*" after an error in quoted material. An editor uses this expression to indicate that the error is in the original. This expression is most often used in literary contexts.

> Mr. Hart said in his article: "The staff is well qualified to make an analyses *[sic]* of prevailing wage rates."

Use brackets as **secondary parentheses** (parentheses within parentheses).

> Remote Control 600 is not standard equipment on Model No. 6789 (see Catalog 94 [Summer 1996] for separate pricing).

Quotation Marks " "

Use quotation marks to enclose the exact words of a speaker or writer.

Separate a simple, one-sentence quotation from its source with a comma or commas.

> Mr. Hamilton said, "We must increase our profits if we are to survive."
> "Please," Dr. Stanton said, "do not decrease our operating room staff."

Separate a longer (two or more sentences) or more formal quote from its source with a colon. Formal quotes are frequently introduced with expressions such as *spoke thus, said in part, as follows, the following,* and *stated.*

> The President continued as follows: "This nation cannot continue on this dangerous course. We must take action now."

> Our architect, Nancy Morrison, wrote: "When one specifies products of fine quality, a $180,000 house will rise in cost by 10 to 25 percent. The higher total cost may make the house more expensive than the neighborhood warrants."

If a direct quotation at the beginning of a sentence is a question or an exclamation , a question mark or an exclamation point is used instead of a comma after the quotation.

> "Will the board meet tomorrow at ten?" Mr. Decker asked.

Do not use quotation marks for indirect quotations.

> He said that he would attend.

A quotation of four or more lines should be presented as a separate paragraph with quotation marks at the beginning and end of the paragraph.

The President spoke to the Cabinet as follows:

"_____

_____

_____

_____."

Consecutive paragraphs of quoted material may be presented in either of two ways:

1. With opening quotation marks at the beginning of each paragraph but with closing quotation marks only at the end of the last paragraph

Here is a transcript of the President's remarks:

"_____

_____

_____

_____.

"_____

_____

_____

_____."

2. Without quotation marks but specially indented from the left and right margins and centered a double space below the preceding paragraph.

Here is a transcript of the President's remarks:

_____

_____

_____

_____

_____

_____

_____

_____

_____

Use **single quotation marks** (' ') for a quotation appearing within another quotation.

"Then I heard her ask, 'Is this the way to Portland?'"

Use **quotation marks** to enclose

Definitions

The prefix _in-_ also means _"not, no, without."_

Slogans, mottoes, or other familiar quotations

"All's well that ends well" was his only comment.

Notations quoted from signs, packages, and papers of various kinds. Each word in these notations is capitalized.

> The letter was returned with *"Address Unknown"* stamped on it.
> Please write *"Paid"* on these bills.

Part of a quotation may be omitted if the omission is indicated by a mark of ellipsis (. . .).

Quotations in relation to other punctuation marks

A period and a comma are always placed inside the closing quotation marks.

> "Your terms are acceptable," he wrote, " with just one exception."

A colon and a semicolon are always placed outside the closing quotation marks.

> The check is marked "Account Closed"; however, I am sure that an error has been made.

A question mark and an exclamation point are placed inside the closing quotation marks if they refer to just the quoted material or if they refer to the quoted material and to the sentence as a whole. Never use one of these marks and a period at the end of a sentence.

> Mr. Barnes asked, "Can you ship the copper tubing this week?"
> How pleased we were to hear you say, "A remarkable achievement!"

A question mark and an exclamation point are placed outside the quotation marks if they refer to the sentence as a whole, <u>but not to the quoted material.</u>

> Did he say, "We consider its styling to be the reason for its success"?

End Punctuation

Exclamation Points
Use an exclamation point after any word, phrase, or clause that expresses **strong feeling:** to express a command, approval, disapproval, admiration, or surprise. In business writing this mark of punctuation is used sparingly.

> By all means, begin at once! (COMMAND)
> Congratulations on your promotion! (APPROVAL)
> The idea! (DISAPPROVAL)
> What a beautiful picture! (ADMIRATION)
> Congratulations! You finished the project ahead of schedule! (SURPRISE)

Periods
Use a period at the end of a sentence that **states a fact, asks an indirect question, gives a command,** or **politely requests an action,** rather than actually expecting an answer.

> The director agreed with your assessment of the problem. (STATEMENT)
> She asked which memo contained the relevant information. (INDIRECT QUESTION)
> Put your requests in my box before noon on Friday. (COMMAND)
> Will you please return the enclosed form before January 15. (REQUEST)
> Please call if I can be of further help. (REQUEST)

Punctuation

A polite request refers to a question to which no direct answer is expected. Phrasing such a request as a question suggests an action. Such requests often begin with *May we, Will you, Won't you.* A question mark is often preferred over a period. When a direct answer to the question is expected, a question mark must be used.

Polite request: Will you please let us have your decision immediately.

Question requiring an answer : May we have our salesman call?

Use a period after each independent clause in a **tabulation or topical outline.** Use a period and two spaces after the number or letter enumerating the list.

A good training program is designed to serve several purposes:
1. It supplements academic training with technical skills.
2. It introduces the trainee to company policies and procedures.

A period is not necessary after any item including the last in a tabulation of words, phrases, or dependent clauses.

These topics will be discussed on March 16:
a. Our fiscal policy
b. The role of taxes
c. Anticipated expenditures

If an abbreviation at the end of a declarative sentence requires a period, only one period is used. At the end of a question or exclamation, an abbreviation requiring a period is followed by a question mark or exclamation point.

Jane Monroe is an M.D.
Is William Monroe an M.D.?
That young man is an M.D.!

Indicate an **ellipsis** (an intentional omission of words) with three spaced periods in succession. Three periods plus the closing mark of punctuation indicate an omission at the end of a sentence.

The speaker remarked, "I am sure that your talents will be exercised to the fullest ... for your own happiness and the welfare of all."

The interviewer asked, "Have you had courses in economics, sociology, business management ... ?"

For additional information on the use of periods with abbreviations, with initials, with decimals, and in lists and topical outlines, see Style, pages 26-31.

Question Marks ?

Use a question mark after **direct requests** for information.

Will you be able to attend next month's meeting?

Do not put a question mark after an indirect question.

I wonder whether he will attend the meeting.

Use a question mark after a **statement intended as a question.**

> You are Mrs. Gregory's assistant?

Use a question mark after each question in a series of **short interrogations,** even if they are elliptical.

> We might ask these questions: Is the product appealing? Is it convincing? Is it reasonably priced?
>
> We might ask these questions: Is the product appealing? Convincing? Reasonably priced?

Use a question mark after an **independent question** that appears within a larger sentence. Capitalize the first word of the question.

> The question Why do homework? sparked a lively discussion.
>
> The question we are left with is What is our next step?

Use a question mark after a **quoted question** within a declarative sentence. The question mark is placed inside the quotation marks because it is part of the quoted material.

> Whenever he asks, "Has anyone seen my keys?" we all groan.

When the sentence, as well as the quote, is a question, the question mark goes outside the closing quotes.

> Were you surprised when he asked, "How soon can you join our staff"?

Use a question mark at the end of a sentence that contains an added or **inserted direct question.**

> You were present for her talk, *weren't you?*
>
> Miss Allison is, *is she not,* a native of England?

Use a question mark enclosed in parentheses to **express doubt** about a preceding word, figure, or statement.

> The two companies merged in 1965 *(?)* and moved to New Jersey.

Use a question mark after a **question** enclosed **in parentheses.**

> His latest book *(did you see the review in last Sunday's Times?)* is selling very well.
>
> On the 29th I will be in Kansas City. *(Will you be in your office on that day?)*

Spacing With Marks of Punctuation

The Period
No spacing after the periods within lowercase abbreviations:
> e.g.   i.e.

No spacing after a decimal point:
> 10.5 percent $15.60

One space after personal initials:

    Mrs. H. B. Houghton

One space at the end of an abbreviation within a sentence:

    Please change her title to Mrs. on all our stationery.

Two spaces after the period at the end of a sentence:

    The meeting will begin at 9 AM. I'll be in the room at 8:45.

Two spaces after the period following a letter or number in a topical outline:

    I. This is the setup for a topical outline:
        A. You cannot have an A. without a B.
        B. A. and B. should both be written in the same grammatical form.
            1. Each new subtopic is indented from the previous one.
            2. Continue with this pattern until the end.

The Comma
No space within numbers:

    16,000 copies $2,345,896

One space after comma within a sentence:

    He will be in the ofice on Monday, Tuesday, and Wednesday.

The Semicolon
One space after the semicolon:

    Later and latest pertain to time; latter and last pertain to position.

The Colon
No space before or after when the colon separates hour from minutes:

    4:40 AM

No space before or after the colon separating identification initials:

    WER:PO

Two spaces after the colon within a sentence:

    One thing is certain: We have run out of time.

Two spaces after the word *Subject* in a subject line:

    Subject: Federal Fiscal Policy.

Two spaces between the main title and subtitle of a publication:

Waterway: A History of the Panama Canal.

Two spaces after the city of publication in a footnote or bibliographic reference:

> Porter G. Perrin, Writer's Guide and Index to English (Glenview, Ill.: Scott, Foresman & Co., 1994), p. 420

The Dash
No space before, between, or after a dash.

> Your supplies—paper, cartridges, and fluid—will be delivered this morning.

Parentheses
One space before the opening parenthesis and one space after the closing parenthesis within a sentence.

No space before or after the parenthetic material inside the parentheses.

> The price (is it $5?) seems reasonable.

Two spaces before the opening parenthesis of an independent parenthetic element.

> All prices have been reduced. (See price list enclosed.)

Quotation Marks
No space between quotation marks and the quoted material or between quotation marks and other marks of punctuation.

One space before and after the marks within a sentence.

> Mr. Martin wrote the article "How Much Is Enough?" in the Ladies' Home Journal.

Question Mark and Exclamation Point
One space after a question mark or an exclamation point within a sentence.

> The booklet *What Is the IRS?* is available now.

Two spaces after a question mark or exclamation point at the end of a sentence.

> How splendid! You did very well.

Proper Names
No space follows such particles as D', O', Mc, Mac.

> D'Elia   O'Donnell   McCall   MacMillan

One space ordinarily follows such particles as De, Des, di, La, Le, Los, Van, Von

> De Soto   di Leo   Des Moines   La Jolla
> Le Brun   Von Braun   Los Angeles   Van Brugh

CHAPTER 4 **Parts of Speech**

CHAPTER 4 # Parts of Speech

Verbs

A verb is a word or words that express mental or physical action.

> MENTAL: They *had pondered* that question all morning.
> PHYSICAL: She *shut* the lights as she *left* the office.

A verb may also help make a statement.

> He *has* the encyclopedia.   The report *is* incomplete.

Verbs have the following characteristics: tense, voice, and mood.

Principal Parts and Tenses

Every verb has four principal parts—the present, the present participle, the past, and the past participle—upon which all tenses and other modifications of the verb are based.

All regular verbs form the past and past participle by adding *d* or *ed* to the present form and form the present participle by adding *ing* to the present.

Present	Past (present+ed)	Past Participle (present+ed)	Present Participle (present+ing)
need	needed	needed	needing
type	typed	typed	typing
walk	walked	walked	walking
drop	dropped	dropped	dropping
estimate	estimated	estimated	estimating
die	died	died	dying
live	lived	lived	living

Many frequently used verbs, however, have principal parts that are irregularly formed.

Present	Past	Past Participle	Present Participle
am, is, are	was, were	been	being
begin	began	begun	beginning
bring	brought	brought	bringing
buy	bought	bought	buying
come	came	come	coming
eat	ate	eaten	eating
give	gave	given	giving
go	went	gone	going
have	had	had	having
lay	laid	laid	laying
lie (recline)	lay	lain	lying
lie (tell a falsehood)	lied	lied	lying
run	ran	run	running
take	took	taken	taking
think	thought	thought	thinking
write	wrote	written	writing

Using the Dictionary. Most dictionaries show the principal part for <u>irregular</u> verbs, even when the irregularity is only the doubling of a consonant.

> **run vi. ran, run, run · ning**
> **drop vi. dropped, drop · ping**

If the verb is regular, the principal parts are not shown.

> **wait vi.**

The past participle and the present participle are used with one or more auxiliary (helping) verbs in a <u>verb phrase</u> (a verb of more than one word).

Auxiliary Verbs

am	is	was	were	be	being	been	
can	could	do	does	did	has	have	had
should	would	may	might	must	shall	will	are

The parts of a verb phrase may be separated from each other in a sentence.

> *Have* you *read* that report?
> She *has* thoroughly *reviewed* the test results.

A verb can have six tenses. Each tense has a <u>progressive form</u>, which is used to indicate a continuing action. In addition, the present and the past have an <u>emphatic form</u> composed of *do, does,* or *did* plus the present form of a verb.

Tense		Progressive	Emphatic
Present	I write	I am writing	I do write
Present Perfect	I have written	I have been writing	
Past	I wrote	I was writing	I did write
Past Perfect	I had written	I had been writing	
Future	I shall (will) write	I shall (will) be writing	
Future Perfect	I shall (will) have written	I shall (will) have been writing	

Formal writing requires the use of *shall* with *I* and *we* to express future time. Informal writing uses *shall* and *will* interchangeably to express future time with *I* and *we*. [See more in "Glossary of Usage," page 151.]

Present tense denotes present time, a habitual action, or an accepted truth. It may also denote future time.

> PRESENT: I *hear* footsteps.
> HABITUAL: He *travels* to work by train.
> ACCEPTED TRUTH: Haste *makes* waste.
> FUTURE: Our ship *departs* tomorrow.

Present Perfect (*has* or *have* + past participle) identifies an action that began in the past and was completed in the present or an action that began in the past and is still continuing.

> COMPLETED: I *have finished* the report.
> CONTINUING: She *has worked* here for 15 years.

Past denotes an action completed in the past.

>Yesterday she *wrote* to several officials about her environmental concerns.

Past Perfect (*had* + past participle) identifies an action that occurred in the past before another past action or event.

>He *had discussed* the problem before he made his decision.

Future (*shall* or *will* + present) denotes an action that will occur at some time in the future.

>Next week they *will paint* the third-floor offices.

Future perfect (*shall* or *will* + *have* + past participle) identifies an action that will occur in the future before another future action or event.

>He *will have gathered* all the data by the time we arrive.

Mood

Verbs have three moods—the indicative, the imperative, and the subjunctive.

Indicative makes a statement or asks a question.

>He *left* early.
>*Did* he *leave* early?

Imperative gives a command or makes a request. The subject of an imperative verb is *you* either expressed or (more often) understood.

>(*You*) Tell them to lock the door when they leave.
>(*You*) Please sign and return the enclosed form.

Subjunctive indicates that an action or condition does not exist in reality. The action or condition is wished for or is dependent on an unrealized factor. Subjunctive is used <u>only</u> in dependent clauses after such words as *wish, if, as if,* and *as though.*

>I felt as if I *were* 17 again. (but I'm not)
>If I *were* in her place, I would accept the promotion. (but I'm not)

The subjunctive also follows a verb or expression indicating necessity, demand, request, urging, or resolution.

>It is necessary that you *be* ready on time.
>He suggested that she *take* the contract home to read carefully.
>The committee has resolved that the suggestion *be tabled.*

Using the subjunctive involves a special form of the verb in the following instances: The present tense of the verb **be**

Present	Indicative	Present	Subjunctive
I am	we are	(that) I be	(that) we be
you are	you are	(that) you be	(that) you be
he is	they are	(that) he be	(that) they be

The past tense of the verb **be**

Past Indicative		Past Subjunctive	
I was	we were	(if) I were	(if) we were
you were	you were	(if) you were	(if) you were
he was	they were	(if) he were	(if) they were

For all other verbs the third person singular of the subjunctive drops the final *s* of the indicative.

Present Indicative	Present Subjunctive
he *works*	(suggested that) he *work*
she *finishes*	(demanded that) she *finish*
it *happens*	(is necessary that) it *happen*

Voice

The voice of the verb indicates whether the subject of the verb is the doer of an action (**active voice**) or the receiver of an action (**passive voice**).

Active Voice	Passive Voice
	(a form of *be* + past participle)
The *judge repeated* the order.	The *order was repeated* by the judge.
She will lead the discussion.	The *discussion will be led* by her.

Active verbs are simpler, less wordy, more direct. Passive verbs typically produce longer and more awkward sentences. Unless you deliberately want to de-emphasize the doer of the action, use verbs in the active voice.

Transitive and Intransitive Verbs

Verbs are also classified as transitive or intransitive. In most dictionaries verbs are labeled either transitive **vt.** or intransitive **vi.** Note that some verbs function both as transitive and intransitive.

A **transitive verb** is one that has a receiver of the action. The noun that receives the action is called the <u>direct object</u>.

He presented his <u>budget</u> last week. (He presented what?)

A verb that has a direct object may also have an <u>indirect object</u>, the person or thing to or for whom the action is done. The indirect object is found between the verb and the direct object.

He gave <u>me</u> the new budget last week. (To whom did he give the budget?)

All verbs in the passive voice are transitive, in which case the subject receives the action.

Our new <u>letterhead</u> was designed by Ann Ames.

<u>Kevin</u> was awarded second prize.

An **intransitive verb** has no receiver of the action. In the same way, linking verbs do not take objects, but are completed by <u>complements</u>. Thus, they are often classified as intransitive.

> She *was standing* near the telephone.
> They *will fly* to Chicago next week.
> Helen *is* our new leader. (*leader* is the complement of *is*)

Troublesome Verbs

See the "Glossary of Usage" (page 130) for the correct use of the following:

accept, except	come, go	may, might
adapt, adopt	compare, contrast	paid, payed
advise, inform	complement, compliment	passed, past
affect, effect	counsel	precede, proceed
envelop, envelope	disburse, disperse	proved, proven
aggravate, irritate	done, don't	raise, rise
appraise, apprise	emigrate, immigrate	recommend, refer
ascent, assent	got, have got to	serve, service
assure, ensure, insure	imply, infer	set, sit
bring, take	lay, lie	shall, should
can, could	leave, let	will, would
cannot	lend, loan	
cite, site	maybe, may be	

Subject-Verb Agreement

A verb must always agree with its subject in person and number.

Person means that the subject can be

> **First Person** = the speaker (I, we)
> **Second Person** = the person spoken to (you, us)
> **Third Person** = the person or thing spoken about (he, she, they, them, it)

Number means that the subject can be

> **Singular:** The *report is* on the desk.
> **Plural:** The *reports are* on the desk.

REMEMBER: Although a noun that ends in *s* is usually <u>plural</u>, a verb that ends in *s* is third person <u>singular</u>.

> **Singular:** The *rule applies* to all students.
> **Plural:** The *rules apply* to all students.

A sentence may be in normal order—that is, with the subject preceding the verb—or in inverted order—the verb preceding the subject. Either way the subject and verb must agree in number. The words *here* and *there* are adverbs and normally are not the subject of the verb.

Does she understand the importance of her job?
Here *are* the *copies* that you requested.
There *go* my *chances* for a raise.
In the top middle drawer *are* two new *cartridges* for the printer.
Unnecessary words are used too often in her writing.

Intervening phrases

The subject of the verb is never found in a prepositional phrase. A phrase that comes between a subject and its verb does not affect agreement.

The *director*, as well as her assistant, *is* well-versed on this contract.
The *books* on the top of the file *have been* very helpful to me.
The sales *reports*, including the last one, *were sent* to you last week.
No one except the board *knows* the outcome of the meeting.
Mr. *Wilson*, in addition to his three employees, *is* at the convention in Omaha.
The *contents*, not the packaging, *are* what we manufacture.

Some constructions require special attention:

A **compound subject** joined by *and* or *both...and* requires a plural verb.

The *director and her staff are* in the conference room.
Mary and her sister go to work together in the morning.

A compound that refers to one person or forms a unit requires a singular verb.

Ham and eggs is my favorite breakfast. (ONE DISH)
His *friend and partner has* an office down the hall. (ONE PERSON)
His *friend and his partner have* offices down the hall. (TWO PERSONS)

When a **compound subject** is joined by *or, either...or, neither...nor,* or *not only...but also,* the verb must agree with the subject closer to it.

Either July or *August is* when vacations are scheduled.
Not only the teachers but also the *students are* unhappy about the change.
Neither he nor *I am* available to meet with you today.
Neither the district managers nor the *administrator* favors the plan.
Neither the administrator nor the *district managers favor* the plan.

When subjects expressing **periods of time, amounts of money, or quantities** represent a total amount, use a singular verb. When these subjects represent individual units, use a plural verb.

Twenty-two dollars is the cost of the product. (SINGULAR)
Thousands of dollars have been wasted on this project. (PLURAL)
Two acres is the minimum you need to build in that area. (SINGULAR)
Two acres were given to the community for a park. (PLURAL)

A **collective noun** is a word that is singular in form but represents a group of persons, animals, or things. Some examples are *committee, herd, council, jury, class, society.*

A collective noun is usually thought of as a single unit and takes a singular verb.

Her *family is* ready to leave on vacation.
The *board of directors meets* every week.
The *committee has agreed* on a new chairperson.

When it is clear that the individual members of the unit are acting as individuals, a plural verb is used.

My *family are* still *arguing* about where to go for dinner.

Indefinite pronouns

The indefinite pronouns *each, every, either, neither, one, another, much* and *many a* are always singular. Whether such a pronoun is used as the subject or as an adjective modifying the subject, the verb must be singular.

Each of the students *is interested* in how to write a resume.
Neither employee *is willing* to work overtime.
One parcel *has been sent* via Federal Express; *another is being readied* now.
Every retailer and wholesaler *has been affected* by the shortage.
Many a day and night *has been spent* working on the project.

The indefinite pronouns *both, few, many, others*, and *several* are always plural. Whether used as the subject or as an adjective modifying the subject, the verb must be plural.

Many are called but *few are chosen*.
Both partners *are* out of town.
Several were asked to lunch; *others were overlooked*.

The indefinite pronouns *all, any, most, none*, and *some* may be singular or plural, depending on the noun they refer to.

All of the exposed employees *are tested* for TB. (PLURAL)
All of the money *was used* for supplies. (SINGULAR)
Most of the packages *were lost*. (PLURAL)
Most of the production run *is* defective. (SINGULAR)
Some of the items *are* too expensive. (PLURAL)
Some of this material *is* of second quality. (SINGULAR)

All other indefinite pronouns are singular and require singular verbs. For a complete list of indefinite pronouns, see page 86.

Every one of us is responsible for cleaning our own desks.
Everyone is waiting for the speaker.
Somebody is taking care of that already.
No one was able to explain the proposal clearly.
Everybody was gone by six o'clock.
Nothing was solved by his extraordinary show of temper.

The expression **the number** is always singular; the expression **a number** is usually plural.

The number of books she has ordered *is* overwhelming. (SINGULAR)
A number of new accountants *have been hired*. (PLURAL)
A number is being supplied by our analyst. (SINGULAR)

A **relative pronoun** agrees with its antecedent (the word it refers to) in person, number, and gender. Choose the verb in an adjective clause based on the number of the noun being modified.

> Ms. Carmody is the executive <u>who</u> <u>is</u> responsible for that department. (SINGULAR)
> Each of the candidates <u>who</u> <u>are</u> waiting has already taken the test. (PLURAL)
> He is the only one of the attorneys <u>who</u> <u>is</u> transferring to Chicago. (SINGULAR)

Names of **business firms; organizations; publications; artistic, literary,** and **musical works;** and **geographic locations** are singular.

> <u>General Motors</u> <u>is</u> the company for which he works.
> I think <u>The New York Times</u> <u>has</u> an excellent book section.
> Holbein's <u>The Ambassadors</u> <u>hangs</u> in London's National Gallery.
> The <u>Netherlands</u> <u>is</u> the first stop on my itinerary.

The number of the noun or pronoun in an "of phrase" (expressed or understood) following a **percentage,** a **portion,** or a **fraction** determines whether the percentage, portion, or fraction takes a singular or plural verb.

> <u>Three-fourths</u> of the employees <u>are</u> fully <u>covered</u> by insurance. (PLURAL *employees*)
> <u>Three-fourths</u> of the medical plan <u>is self-insured.</u> (SINGULAR *plan*)
> The <u>majority</u> of our executives <u>are required</u> to contribute to their pension plan. (PLURAL *executives*)

Note that a **phrase** or a **clause** used as the subject of a sentence takes a singular verb.

> <u>Whether he won or lost the contest</u> <u>does</u> not matter. (NOUN CLAUSE)
> <u>Whomever you support</u> <u>is</u> likely to win the election. (NOUN CLAUSE)
> <u>Analyzing the financial data</u> <u>takes</u> a great deal of my time. (GERUND PHRASE)

Check your dictionary or see Plurals, page 104, for rules covering foreign nouns, nouns ending in *ics,* nouns with the same form in the singular and plural, and nouns ending in *s.*

Nouns

A noun is a word that names a person, place, thing, or idea.

Kinds of Nouns

A **proper noun** is the name of a particular person, place, or thing. A proper noun is always capitalized.

> John W. Harris   Mexico City   Empire State Building

A **common noun** is the general name of a person, place, or thing. There are two kinds of common nouns: concrete and abstract.

Concrete nouns name something that can be perceived by the senses.

> book   flower   river   house

Abstract nouns name a quality or idea.

charity	intelligence	devotion	respect

Collective nouns name a group of persons, places, or things.

jury	committee	flock	nation

Compound nouns are nouns with two or more words. Both common and proper nouns may be compound.

Atlantic City	sales tax	brother-in-law

Troublesome Nouns

See the "Glossary of Usage" (page 131) for the correct use of the following:

advice, advise	compliments	lend, loan
affect, effect	consensus	loss
all ways	consul, council, counsel	media
allusion, illusion	data	personal, personnel
alumnus, alumni	descent, dissent	principal, principle
alumna, alumnae	envelop, envelope	sight, site
amount, number	everyday, every day	someday, some day
ascent, assent	foreword, forward	sometime, some time
balance	kind, sort, type	stationary, stationery
capital, capitol	lead, led	weather, whether

Pronouns

A pronoun is a word used in place of a noun or another pronoun to avoid having to constantly repeat the same word. The noun or the pronoun being replaced is called the <u>antecedent</u>.

AWKWARD: Mary finished all Mary's work before Mary went home.
IMPROVED: Mary finished all <u>her</u> work before <u>she</u> went home.
(*Her* and *she* are pronouns; their antecedent is *Mary*.)

AWKWARD: Will everyone please check everyone's portfolio.
IMPROVED: Will everyone please check <u>his</u> or <u>her</u> portfolio.
(*His* and *her* are pronouns; their antecedent is *everyone*.)

All pronouns have these characteristics: person, number, gender, case.

Person

First person = the person speaking—I, me, my, mine, we, our, ours, us.

Second person = the person spoken to—you, your, yours

Third person = the person or thing spoken about—he, she, it, his, her, hers, its, him, they, their, theirs, them.

Number

The <u>number</u> of a pronoun indicates whether a pronoun is either singular or plural.

Do all the students have <u>their</u> lunches?
(*Their* is the pronoun; *students* is its antecedent.)
Some term papers have not been collected; do all students present have <u>theirs</u>?

Gender

The <u>gender</u> of nouns and pronouns refers to their classification according to sex.

Gender	Sex	Examples
masculine	male	John, man, he
feminine	female	Sally, woman, she
common	either	citizen, student
neuter	none	house, machine, it

A pronoun must agree with its antecedent in person, number, and gender.

<u>Ms. Smith</u> was sure *her* proposal would be approved.
<u>John</u> said *he* is willing to chair the committee.
The <u>committee</u> has given no indiciation that *it* will make any recommendations.
Should <u>I</u> take *my* raincoat with me?
<u>Harry and Louise</u> donated *theirs* to charity.
<u>Neither José nor Abdul</u> volunteered *his* services.

When a common noun is the antecedent, the question of which pronoun to use may arise. Tradition has dictated that it be masculine, but this practice has lost favor because of its sexist implications. Instead you can

refer to both sexes: I hope every teacher will send me *his* or *her* reports.
make the antecedent plural: I hope all teachers will send me *their* reports.
eliminate the pronoun: I hope every teacher will send me reports.

Be especially careful not to stereotype people such as doctors, professors, lawyers, bosses, and employers as male and people such as secretaries, teachers, and nurses as female.

SEXIST: A doctor should give his patients thorough care.
BETTER: Doctors should give their patients thorough care.

SEXIST: A nurse needs to upgrade her license every five years.
BETTER: Nurses need to upgrade their licenses every five years.

The antecedent to which a pronoun refers should immediately be clear to the reader.

INCORRECT: The benefits are excellent. They said they pay for full medical coverage.

Who are they? Either give *they* an antecedent, or replace it with a noun.

CORRECT: Mrs. Bronson assured me that the benefits are excellent. *She* said the company pays for full medical benefits.

She clearly refers to Mrs. Bronson.

Parts of Speech

The antecedent must be a noun or another pronoun, not an entire clause.

INCORRECT:	The train was delayed, which caused our late arrival.
CORRECT:	The train delay caused our late arrival.

INCORRECT:	I arrived at work two hours late. This infuriated my employer.
CORRECT:	My arrival at work two hours late infuriated my employer.
CORRECT:	My employer was furious because I arrived at work two hours late.

Case

The three cases—nominative, objective, possessive—indicate how the noun or pronoun functions in relation to other words in a sentence. Pronouns, unlike nouns, change form when they change case.

Nominative: *I* called Mary.
Objective: Mary called *me.*
Possessive: She has *mine;* I have *hers.*

Kinds of Pronouns
Personal Pronouns

Personal pronouns, except *it*, refer to persons. They change form as they change case.

	Nominative	Possessive	Objective
First person singular	I	my, mine	me
Second person singular	you	your, yours	you
Third person singular	he, she, it	his, her, hers, its	him, her, it
First person plural	we	our, ours	us
Second person plural	you	your, yours	you
Third person plural	they	their, theirs	them

Never confuse possessive pronouns, which <u>never</u> have apostrophes, with contractions such as *it's* (it is), *there's* (there is or was), *you're* (you are), *they're* (they are).

Use the **nominative case** for the following positions in a clause:

When the pronoun is the subject of a verb

He needs to finish this report by tomorrow.
Mrs. Lopez and *I will attend* the convention.

When the pronoun is the complement of a linking verb.

It was *I* who set the date for the meeting.
Was it *she* who phoned for an appointment?

Use the **objective case** for the following positions in a clause:

When the pronoun is the complement of an action verb.

Ms. Davis gave *us* the budget to review. (INDIRECT OBJECT OF gave)
The supervisor questioned Louis and *me* at length. (DIRECT OBJECT OF thanked)

When the pronoun is the object of a preposition.

> She gave the report to *me.*
> The members were all on time except *you* and *me.*
> Between *you* and *me,* I know I am the best technician in our laboratory.

When the pronoun is the subject, complement or object of an infinitive. (See the discussion of *to be*, treated separately below.)

> We asked *him* to head the committee
> Did you ask *her* to play *me* in the skit?
> Did you remember to call *her?*

When the pronoun is part of a compound subject of a gerund.

> I don't like my daughter and *him* staying out so late.

To be, a linking infinitive, takes the same case before it and after it. When a *to be* infinitive has a subject, the complement is in the objective case to match the subject of the infinitive.

> They took *her* to be *me.* (*her* is the subject of *to be; me,* the complement)

When *to be* doesn't have a subject, the complement is in the nominative case to match the subject of the verb.

> The intruder pretended to be *he.*

If correct, you should always be able to reverse the elements of such a sentence.

> *He* pretended to be the intruder.
> They took me to be her.

Use the **possessive case** in the following positions in a clause:

> When the pronoun is used as an adjective showing possession either before the noun or as the complement of a linking verb.

> > It was *my* job that the company eliminated.
> > The choice is *yours.*

> When the pronoun is the only subject of a gerund.

> > I should appreciate *your* letting me know by Friday.

When the pronoun follows *than* or *as* in a comparison, supply the missing words and then choose the case accordingly.

> She types better than *I.* (than I type)
> I like you better than *him.* (than I like him)
> Ms. Larson is not as good at algebra as *she.* (as she is)

When a pronoun is used as an appositive, its case is the same as that of its antecedent.

> Two secretaries, Sally and *I,* were asked to attend the class. (BOTH NOMINATIVE)
> The instructions were given to the new employees, Sally and *me.* (BOTH OBJECTS OF PREPOSITION *to*)

In sentences like these mentally simplify to determine the correct form.

Sally and *I* were asked to attend the class.

The instructions were given to *me*.

Compound Personal Pronouns

Singular   **Plural**

myself   itself   ourselves
yourself himself   yourselves
herself   themselves

These pronouns have two uses:

To **emphasize** a noun or pronoun already expressed.

I *myself* don't understand the problem.
Carol completed the project *herself.*

To **reflect** the action of the verb back to the subject.

Ann prepared *herself* for the interview.
They insured *themselves* against product liability.

A compound personal pronoun <u>must</u> have an antecedent within the sentence.

INCORRECT: He spoke to Ann and *myself.*
CORRECT: He spoke to Ann and *me.*

Interrogative Pronouns

Interrogative pronouns ask questions. Only *who* changes form as it changes case.

Nominative	**Possessive**	**Objective**
who	whose	whom
what		what
which		which

Who has already completed the assignment?
Whom do you want to see?
Whose was stolen?
Which typewriter needs a new ribbon?
What did he want?

Relative Pronouns

Relative pronouns introduce noun and adjective clauses. The pronouns *who* and *whoever* change form as they change case.

Nominative	**Possessive**	**Objective**
who, whoever, whosoever	whose, whosever	whom, whomever
that		that
what, whatever		what, whatever
which, whichever		which, whichever

I don't know *who* completed the assignment.
He wants to interview the student *whom* you recommended.
She interviewed the students *whose work was finished.*
They give help to *whoever* needs it.

Who, the nominative case, should be used whenever *he* can be substituted in the clause. *Whom*, the objective case, should be used whenever *him* can be substituted. One trick is to mentally answer the implied question to determine the correct case.

Who shall we say interviewed us.? (*He* interviewed us.)
The matter of *who* should go has not been decided. (*He* should go)
We will choose *whoever* is best suited for the job. (*He* is best suited)
Mr. Varis is the one *who* we think will be chosen. (We think *he* will be chosen)
Give the package to *whoever* comes for it. (*He* comes for it.)

Whom did you see for the interview? (I saw *him*)
To *whom* were you talking? (I was talking to *him*)
It depends on *whom* you talk to. (I talked to *him*)
We need a manager *whom* we can trust. (We can trust *him*)
He is the candidate *whom* we intend to support. (We intend to support *him*.)
Whom did you take him to be? (I took *him* to be John)

In general use *that* for essential adjective clauses and *which* for nonessential adjective clauses.

The firm *that has just been acquired* will be a great asset to us.
Wonderful Widgets, *which we have just acquired,* will be a wonderful asset.

If the word *that* has already been used in the sentence, use *which* for an essential adjective clause.

We understand *that* the firm *which* we just acquired will be a great asset.

Use *who* and *whom* to refer to persons.

Mr. Bell is the man *who* I believe is chairperson.
Ms. Jones is the woman *whom* we saw in the store.

For the punctuation of essential and nonessential adjective clauses, see pages 52-54.

Demonstrative Pronouns

Demonstrative pronouns indicate particular persons, places, or things.

Singular	Plural
this	these
that	those

That is not the book I recommended to you.
These are much too expensive for our budget.

Indefinite Pronouns

Indefinite pronouns substitute for an unspecified person, place, or thing.

Singular Indefinite Pronouns

another (another's)   either (either one's)   one another (one another's)
anybody (anybody's)   everyone (everyone's)   one (one's)
anyone (anyone's)   everything   other (other's)
anyone else (anyone else's) neither (neither one's)   somebody (somebody's)
anything   no one (no one's)   someone (someone's)
each   someone else (someone else's)
each one (each one's)   something
each other (each other's)

> *Neither* of the accountants finished his report.
> Does *either* of you need help?
> Proofread *one another's* work.

These pronouns often call for the generic use of *he, him,* or *his.*   Although perfectly correct grammatically, you may find it better to reword to avoid appearing sexist.

RATHER THAN: *Everyone* should submit *his* report by May 1.
USE: All department *heads* should submit *their* reports by May 1.

Use *one* in an impersonal reference. Use *you* in direct personal reference.

IMPERSONAL: *One* may obtain a credit card at this office.
PERSONAL: *You* may call me whenever you have a question.

Plural Indefinite Pronouns
both   few   other   several   many

> *Many* have already left for the day; *others* stayed behind.
> *Few* understood the importance of the merger.

Singular or Plural Indefinite Pronouns
all   any   most   none   some

These indefinite pronouns can be used in the singular or plural depending on their antecedents. The *of phrase* that follows indicates the number.

> *All* of the girls have handed in their assignments.
> *All* of the money was missing.
> *Some* of the people are finding it hard to make ends meet.
> *Some* of the time was spent discussing the proposal.

Troublesome Pronouns

See the "Glossary of Usage" (page 132) for the correct use of the following pronouns:

all, all of   everyone, every one   someone, some one
anyone, any one   it, there   their, there, they're
both   its, it's   who, whom
each other, one another   most   whose, who's
                             nobody   your, you're

Adjectives

Adjectives modify nouns and pronouns by describing, limiting, or identifying them. They answer such questions as Which one? What kind? How many?

> The *tweed* suit would be perfect for work. [What kind of suit?]
> I need *three* copies of the report. [How many copies?]
> Do you want *this* report? [Which report?]

Kinds of Adjectives

Proper adjectives are derived from proper nouns and are capitalized.

> *French* and *American* flags are red, white, and blue.

Coordinate adjectives modify the same noun equally and separately. If you reverse two coordinate adjectives or place *and* between them, the sentence will still read smoothly.

> She is the most *intelligent, articulate* student in the class. (intelligent *and* articulate)

Noncoordinate adjectives do not modify a noun equally and separately. If you insert *and* between them or reverse them, the sentence sounds awkward.

> The company has a *new medical insurance* plan. (not new *and* medical)

For the punctuation of coordinate and noncoordinate adjectives, see page 48.

Words usually classified as other parts of speech are regularly used as adjectives. Remember, it is the function of a word in a particular sentence that determines its part of speech.

> She is working in her *office.* [office IS A NOUN]
> Our *office* machines are serviced by Acme. [office IS AN ADJECTIVE]
> *Either* would be acceptable. [either IS A PRONOUN]
> *Either* plan would be acceptable. [either IS AN ADJECTIVE]

A **compound adjective** consists of two or more words that are combined, with or without hyphens, to form a one-thought modifier. Many, but not all, are in the dictionary.

> a *first-class* seat   a *lifetime* gift   an *awe-inspiring* sight

See Compound Words, page 107.

The articles *a, an,* and *the* are classified as adjectives because they are used to modify nouns. The indefinite articles *a* and *an* are used when the reference is not to any specific object. The definite article *the* refers to a specific object.

> Have you found *a* site for the office building? [NO SPECIFIC SITE]
> Is this *the* site for the new building? [A SPECIFIC SITE]

Parts of Speech

Placement of Adjectives

An adjective may precede or follow the noun it modifies. An adjective may follow a linking verb or follow a direct object as an objective complement.

> PRECEDING THE NOUN: *Fresh* produce is always the best.
> AFTER THE NOUN: All produce, *fresh* or *frozen*, is shipped promptly.
> AFTER A LINKING VERB: She was *sad* to see him leave.
> AFTER THE DIRECT OBJECT: He held the ruler *straight.*.

For the punctuation of essential and nonessential adjectives, see page 56.

Comparison of Adjectives

Most adjectives have three degrees of comparison: positive, comparative, superlative.

Positive degree is the simple form of an adjective and is used to describe, not compare.

> The rug is *wide*.　　　　A *clear* copy is what we need.

Comparative degree is used when two items are compared with each other. Form the comparative degree by adding *er* to all one-syllable adjectives and two-syllable adjectives that end in *y*. Insert *more* or *less* before two-syllable adjectives that don't end in *y* and all adjectives of three or more syllables..

> The blue rug is *wider* than the white one.
> Her house is the *more modern* of the two.
> That color is *less flattering* than the other one.
> She is *prettier* than her sister.

Superlative degree is used when three or more items are compared. Form the superlative degree by adding *est* to all one-syllable adjectives and two-syllable adjectives that end in *y*. Insert *most* or *least* before two-syllable adjectives that don't end in *y* and all adjectives of three or more syllables.

> The gray rug is the *widest* of the three.
> Of the five rugs the red one is the *most colorful.*
> This rug is the *least durable* of all the rugs we stock.

A few adjectives have irregular comparisons, as illustrated here:

Positive	Comparative	Superlative
cheap	cheaper	cheapest
fast	faster	fastest
beautiful	more beautiful	most beautiful
perfect	more nearly perfect	most nearly perfect
good	better	best
well	better	best
much	more	most
many	more	most

Using the Dictionary. When an adjective or adverb has irregular comparative forms, most dictionaries list them after the entry word.

> **good　adj. bet·ter, best**

When the comparative forms are regular, most dictionaries do not list them.

> **cheap　adj.**

Some adjectives, from their very meanings, cannot be compared. They are complete in their simple form, the positive degree. The only comparison possible is formed by using *more nearly* or *most nearly* before the positive degree. Such adjectives include the following:

correct	empty	inferior	round	straight
dead	full	perfect	square	unique
different	universal	wrong		

When an item is compared in the comparative degree with the <u>members of the same group or class</u>, use the word *other* or *else* in the second part of the comparison.

>This rug is wider than *any other* rug in stock.
>He has been more outspoken than *anyone else* in the group.

>**but**

>Detroit, Michigan, is larger than *any* city in Iowa.
>(Detroit is not a city in Iowa.)

When an item is compared in the superlative degree with <u>members of the same class or group</u>, *all* is used.

>This dictionary is the *best of all* I have used.
>*Of all* the courses I took, American Government was the *most interesting*.

Only nouns with comparable qualities can be compared.

>Our profits are higher than they were last year.
>Our profits are higher than those of last year.
>Our profits are higher than last year's. (last year's *profits*)

>INCORRECT: Our profits are higher than last year.
>Illogical because *profits* and *year* are not comparable.

Troublesome Adjectives

See the Glossary of Usage page 130 for the correct use of the following:

a, an	different	illicit
adverse, averse	disinterested, uninterested	ingenious, ingenuous
anxious, eager	eminent, immanent, imminent	last, late, latest
bad, badly	everyday	personal
biannual, biennial	farther, further	principal
bimonthly	fewer, less, lesser	quiet, quite
capital	good, well	real, sure
credible, creditable	healthful, healthy	stationary, stationery

Adverbs

An adverb modifies a verb, a verbal, an adjective, or another adverb.

An adverb usually answers one of these questions: How? When? Where? To what degree? Phrases and clauses used as adverbs also answer the questions Why? and Under what circumstances?

He finished the project *quickly.* [HOW?]
She wanted to go *downtown.* [WHERE?]
She speaks *very* clearly. [TO WHAT DEGREE?]
I'll see you *tomorrow.* [WHEN?]
I joined the health club *to lose weight..* [WHY?]
If I have to stay late, I'll call you. [UNDER WHAT CIRCUMSTANCES?]

Kinds of Adverbs

An **independent adverb** is used to modify the sentence thought. It is usually separated from the rest of the sentence by a comma.

Yes, I will finish by 3 PM.
Truthfully, I was not happy with their decision.

For punctuation of introductory and nonessential adverbs, see pages 52 and 56.

An **interrogative adverb** at the beginning of the sentence asks a question.

How did you arrive at that conclusion?
When will you finish that report?
Why didn't you mail that letter?

A **relative adverb** introduces an adjective clause and modifies the verb in that clause.

This is the house *where* I was born.

Where I was born is an adjective clause modifying house; *where* modifies *was born.*

Correlative adverbs are used in pairs as a connective for adverbial clauses.

Miss Lacy is *as* cooperative *as* she can be.
I am *so* tired *that* I can't think.

See adverbial clause conjunctions, page 92.

Words usually classified as nouns are regularly used as adverbs. Remember, it is the function of the word in a particular sentence that determines its part of speech.

I am ready to go *home.* [WHERE?]
The meeting took place *Monday.* [WHEN?]

Placement of Adverbs

Such adverbs as *almost, also, even, exactly, just, merely, nearly, only, scarcely,* and *too* should be placed before the word they modify in order to avoid ambiguity.

We painted *only* two offices. [no more than two}
Only we painted the two offices. [no one else]
We *only* painted the two offices. [We didn't wallpaper]

Comparison of Adverbs

The rules for forming the comparative and superlative degrees of adverbs are the same as those for adjectives. (See page 88.) Some adverbs have irregular comparative forms.

Positive	Comparative	Superlative
hard	harder	hardest
clearly	more (or less) clearly	most (or least) clearly
early	earlier	earliest
ill	worse	worst
little	less	least
much	more	most
well	better	best

As with adjectives some adverbs cannot be compared. Some examples are

completely	conclusively	hardly	perfectly	there
scarcely	universally	always	never	very

-ly Adverbs

The suffix -ly is often added to an adjective to form an adverb.

Adjective	Adverb
bad	badly
direct	directly
easy	easily
real	really
sure	surely

Many adverbs do not end in ly—for example, *fast, here, near, there, very, too, well*. Not all *ly*-ending words are adverbs. Some are adjectives—for example, *friendly, lovely, manly, cowardly, scholarly*—which are formed by adding *-ly* to a noun.

Troublesome Adverbs

See the "Glossary of Usage" page 130 for the correct usage of the following:

already	differently	most
altogether	farther, further	quite
always	first	really, surely
anymore, any more	foreword, forward	respectfully, respectively
anyplace	formally, formerly	someday, some day
anywhere	good, well	sometime, sometimes
anyway	hopefully	than, then
awhile, a while	late	there
badly	maybe, may be	up
continually, continuously	more importantly	

Conjunctions

A <u>conjunction</u> is a word that connects by joining words, phrases, and clauses to each other.

> Carol *and* Ann will attend the convention. (WORDS)
> Today I went to the bank *and* to the library. (PHRASES)
> Last week we went to New York, *and* next week we will go to Boston. (CLAUSES)
> I will meet you for dinner *if* I have the time.
> (CONNECTS DEPENDENT TO INDEPENDENT CLAUSE)

Coordinate Conjunctions

A **coordinate conjunction** joins words, phrases, or clauses <u>of the same kind.</u>

> CORRECT: She likes <u>swimming</u> *and* <u>fishing</u>. gerunds)
>   She likes <u>to swim</u> *and* <u>to fish</u>. (infinitives)
>
> INCORRECT: She likes <u>swimming</u> *and* <u>to fish</u>.

Below are listed coordinate conjunctions, used singly or in pairs, to join two or more words, phrases, or clauses <u>of the same kind.</u>

and	but	both...and	neither...nor
nor	or	not only...but also	either...or

For punctuation of series, see page 46. For punctuation of compound sentences, see page 47.

Subordinate Conjunctions

A <u>subordinate conjunction</u> connects a dependent clause to an independent clause and shows the relationship between the two. Some subordinate conjunctions are used to connect only one kind of clause; others may be used with more than one.

Commonly Used Subordinate Conjunctions

Adjective Clause Conjunctions			
	who	that	when
	whom	which	where
	whose	why	as

Noun Clause Conjunctions			
	who	that	how
	whoever	what	when
	whom	whatever	where
	whomever	whether	why
	whose	which	
	whosever	whichever	

Adverbial Clause Conjunctions

Comparison:	as...as	so...as	so...that	than
Concession:	although	except for the fact that		
	despite	no matter how, what, when, who		
	even though	however few, many, little		
	even if	in spite of the fact that		
		regardless of what, which, when, where		

Condition:	as long as	if	in case that	on condition that
	provided that	unless	whatever	whether
Contrast:	whereas	only to find that		
Manner:	as	as if	as though	that
Place:	where	wherever		
Purpose:	that	so that	so...that	
Reason:	as	because	inasmuch as	in order that
	since	so that		
Result:	so that	so...that	that	
Time:	after	as	as long as	as often as
	as soon as	before	once	since
	when	whenever	while	until

Conjunctive Adverbs

A <u>conjunctive adverb</u> connects two independent clauses and shows the relationship between them.

Commonly Used Conjunctive Adverbs

accordingly	furthermore	moreover	then
also	hence	nevertheless	therefore
besides	however	otherwise	thus
consequently	likewise	still	yet

I wanted to be there; *however*, we had an emergency at home.
We received the grant; *therefore*, you may proceed with the project
He has failed in the past; *yet* he keeps on trying.

For punctuation of compound sentences, see page 47.

Troublesome Conjunctions

See the Glossary of Usage (page 130) for the correct use of the following:

although, whereas, while	but...however	so, so that
as	if, whether	than, then
as, like	provided, providing	
being as, being that	reason is that	

Prepositions

A <u>preposition</u> is a word that shows the relationship between its object and some other word in the sentence.

Put the box *under* the table.
Put the box *on* the table.
Put the box *near* the table.

In the above sentences *table* is the object of the preposition. The preposition shows the relationship between the *box* and the *table*.

Prepositional Phrases

A <u>phrase</u> is a group of words without a subject and a verb that may be used as an adjective, adverb, or noun. A <u>prepositional phrase</u> consists of a preposition, its object, and any modifiers of the object. The object may be a noun or a pronoun; it may also be a verbal, a phrase, or a clause used as a noun.

Commonly Used Prepositions

about	behind	✓except	off	till
above	below	for	on	to
across	beneath	from	onto	toward
after	beside	in	out	under
against	besides	inside	outside	underneath
along	✓between	into	over	unlike
amid	beyond	less	past	until
among	but	✓like	plus	up
around	by	minus	✓regarding	upon
~~as~~	concerning	near	~~since~~	via
at	despite	notwithstanding	through	with
before	✓during	of	throughout	within, without

Compound Prepositions
(also called phrasal prepositions)

according to	by reason of	in regard to	pertaining to
ahead of	contrary to	in spite of	referring to
along with	except for	instead of	regardless of
apart from	for the sake of	in view of	relating to
as to	in accordance with	irrespective of	relative to
aside from	in addition to	on account of	together with
because of	in connection with	out of	with respect to
by means of	in place of	owing to	

Prepositions with various kinds of objects (the prepositional phrase is underlined; the object is in italics):

NOUN:	The book <u>on the *desk*</u> is yours.
PRONOUN:	Every one <u>of *us*</u> is here.
PREPOSITIONAL PHRASE:	He stepped <u>from *across the aisle*</u>.
GERUND PHRASE:	<u>By *flying to Denver*</u>, you can save time.
INFINITIVE PHRASE:	We have no choice <u>except *to give in*</u>.
NOUN CLAUSE:	Give the box <u>to *whoever calls for it*</u>.

Punctuation of prepositional phrases, see pages 50 and 55.

Idiomatic Prepositions

Common usage requires that certain words be followed by certain prepositions. Some of the common combinations are listed below.

accompanied

by a person	She was accompanied *by* her son.
with a thing	He accompanied his lecture *with* slides.

account
    for an action   He has not been able to account *for* his absence.
    to a person   You will have to account *to* your supervisor.

adapt
    for (made suitable)   The room was adapted *for* storage.
    from (patterned after)   That play was adapted *from* a novel.
    to (change)   She quickly adapted *to* her new job.

agree
    in (be alike or similar)   They agree *in* their basic principles.
    on or *upon* (reach an   The city and the union have agreed *on* the contract.
    understanding)
    to (consent)   Everyone present agreed *to* accompany us.
    with (be in accord)   Our sales projections agree *with* yours.

angry
    with a person   He was very angry *with* the negotiators.
    at or *about* a situation.   He was very angry *about* his demotion.

apply
    for a position   He applied *for* the job of supervisor.
    to someone or something You must apply yourself *to* the job at hand.

argue
    about something   They argued *about* the terms of the agreement.
    with a person   She argued *with* her mother about her curfew.

authority
    for (one who is the source Who is the authority *for* those statistics?
    of a statement or idea)
    on (one who has a claim to He is an authority *on* nuclear physics.
    be believed)
    over (power to command) He has authority *over* this project.

capacity
    for (ability)   These students have a great capacity *for* learning.
    of (content or space)   The seating capacity *of* the auditorium is 1200.

compare
    to (liken; represent   Oak is often compared *to* iron because of
    as similar)   its strength and endurance.
    with (compare, either as Compare this amount *with* the amount shown in
    similar or different)   your checkbook.

concur
    in (be in agreement)   The members of the council concurred *in* their
                      opinion.
    with a person   I concur *with* you that a settlement should be made.

confer
    about (talk about)   The agents will confer *about* the situation in May.
    upon (bestow an honor) The Medal of Honor was conferred *upon* the
                      brave servicemen.

convenient
    for (suitable)   What time is most convenient *for* you?
    to (near)   The office is convenient *to* transportation.

correspond
    to (agree with; resemble; be equal to)
    with (communicate by writing)

Be sure the amount shown on your check corresponds *to* that on the stub.
My attorney has been corresponding *with* them for some time.

differ
    from (be unlike)
    in, over, about (disagree)
    with a person

California differs *from* Florida in many ways.
We seldom differ *over* office procedures.
The stockholders differed *with* the chairman about the direction of the company.

different from
    (<u>never</u> different than)

The number on the check is different *from* that on the stub.

disappointed
    by or *in* someone

    with something

We were disappointed *by* your representative, who failed to attend the meeting.
We were disappointed *with* the results of the vote.

entrust
    something *to* someone
    someone *with* something

He entrusted the report *to* his assistant.
I gladly entrust my entire staff *with* this information.

liable
    for an action
    to someone

The company is liable *for* the action of its agents.
They were liable *to* their employer for loss of time.

speak, talk
    to (implies a monologue)

    with (implies an exchange of ideas)

I will talk *to* you about that later. (You will only listen.)
She wants to speak *with* me about next week's seminar.

Miscellaneous Idiomatic Prepositions

absolve *from*
abstain *from*
accede *to*
acquiesce *in* , *to*
acquit *of*
averse *to*
agreeable *to*
analogous *to*
appreciation *of* or *for*
appreciative *of*
aptitude *for*
at variance *with*
aversion *to*

coincident *with*
compatible *with*
comply *with*
conducive *to*
conform *to*
connect *with*
conversant *with*
deficient *in*
dependent *on*
desist *from*
deter *from*
devoid *of*
dissuaded *from*

graduate *from, of*
identical *with*
in compliance *with*
in conformity *with*
incongruous *with*
incorporated *in*
independent *of*
indifferent *to*
inferior *to*
instill *in, into*
interested *in*
monopoly *of*
necessity *of, for*

need *of, for*
negligent *of*
oblivious *of*
occasion *for*
persistent *in*
preparatory *to*
prerequisite *to*
prior *to*
provided *for*
retroactive *to*
worthy *of*
plan *to*

Problems With Prepositions

Omit prepositions that do not add to the meaning of the sentence.

Where were you ?	not	Where were you *at*?
Where are you going ?	not	Where are you going *to*?
The tickets are inside the envelope.	not	...inside *of* the envelope.
The cartons fell off the truck.	not	...off *of* the truck.
He could not help smiling.	not	...help *from* smiling.
My office is opposite hers.	not	...opposite *to* hers.
I am so glad it is over.	not	...over *with*.

When the same preposition is correct for two different words joined by a conjunction, the preposition is placed after the second word.

> He has respect and admiration *for* the chairman.
> She has an appreciation and knowledge *of* music.

When each word requires a different preposition, be sure to use both prepositions.

> He has neither an aptitude *for* nor an interest *in* politics.
> We have confidence *in* and respect *for* your abilities.

At one time it was considered improper to end a sentence with a preposition. Current usage, however, dictates that this rule be relaxed in favor of achieving a natural-sounding style. Whether or not a sentence should end with a preposition depends on the degree of formality you wish to achieve and on the emphasis desired.

> AWKWARD: I don't know *about* what this is.
> NATURAL: I don't know what this is *about*.
>
> AWKWARD: We need tools *with* which to work.
> NATURAL: We need tools to work *with*.

Avoid ending a sentence with a preposition if doing so is unnecessary and awkward.

> AVOID: Whom are you talking to?
> PREFERRED: To whom are you talking?

For the correct usage of the following troublesome prepositions, see the Glossary of Usage page 130.

at, about	in regard to
among, between	on, onto, on to
as, like	per, a
because of, due to	prior to
beside, besides	

Interjections

An <u>interjection</u> is a word that expresses some abrupt or momentary emotion. It is followed by a comma or an exclamation point, since an interjection has no grammatical connection to the sentence.

> Well, try a different approach!
> Help! We can't balance our books until you send us your payment.

Verbals

Closely related to the parts of speech are the three verbals: the participle, the gerund, and the infinitive. Although verbals derive from verbs, they are not used as verbs but as other parts of speech. Verbals do, however, retain certain properties of verbs:

> They express action, possession, or state of being.
> They may have subjects, complements, and modifiers.
> They have tense and voice.

Participles

A participle is a verbal adjective. It describes or identifies a noun or pronoun by indicating its action or state of being. Participles end in *ed, en,* or *ing.*

> The students *studying for exams* missed the party.

Which students missed the party? The ones studying for exams. *Studying for exams* is a participial phrase that identifies the students.

> *Hurrying to class,* Ann lost her wallet.

Hurrying to class is a participial phrase that describes Ann.

Participles have both tense and voice:

	Present	**Past**	**Perfect**
Active	helping	—	having helped
Passive	being helped	helped	having been helped

The present participle describes action that occurs at the same time as the main verb.

> *Dashing down the stairs,* the student dropped her books.

The past and perfect participles describe action that occurred before the action of the verb.

> *Having finished the report,* she felt free to go to lunch.

Do not use a participle to express purpose or result. A participle is an adjective. Expressing purpose and result is the job of an adverb.

> INCORRECT: We studied for 15 hours, *assuring that we would do well.*
> CORRECT: We studied for 15 hours *because we wanted to do well.*

Independent participial phrases.   An independent participial phrase usually begins with an expression such as *allowing for, considering, granted that,* or *speaking of* and is used to name a general action without reference to a specific performer or receiver of the action indicated.

> *Granted that stock prices are low,* the economy seems buoyant.
> *Speaking of imported goods,* the fall collection at Harrod's is attractive.

Participial absolutes.   A participial absolute consists of a noun or pronoun (the subject of the participle) plus a participle and is grammatically independent of the rest of the sentence. It is related in thought but not in structure to the rest of the sentence.

> *Weather permitting,* we will go to the beach.
> They did very well with the new contract, *all things considered.*

For the punctuation of introductory participial phrases and nonessential participial phrases, see Punctuation, pages 50 and 55.

Gerunds

A gerund is a verbal noun. It names an action. Gerunds always end in *ing*. They can be used anywhere a noun can be used—that is, as a subject, complement, object of a preposition, appositive, etc.

> *Swimming* is an excellent form of exercise.
> She enjoys *playing tennis and golf.*
> *Fighting* did not solve their problem.

Gerunds have both tense and voice:

	Present	**Perfect**
Active	telling	having told
Passive	being told	having been told

The present form of the gerund names an action that occurs at the same time as the action of the main verb.

> *Telling her the answers* is not helping her.
> *Being told the answers* is not helpful.

The perfect form of the gerund names an action that occurred before the action of the verb.

> *His having spoken many times before* prepared him for their questions.
> She regrets *having been misrepresented.*

When it isn't clear whether an *ing* verbal is a participle or a gerund, follow these guidelines:

If the emphasis is on the action, the verbal is a gerund.

> I don't like Ann's *cooking.* (emphasis on *cooking*)
> His *talking* distracted the audience. (emphasis on *talking*)

If the emphasis is on the person, the verbal is a participle.

> I took a picture of Paul *standing* next to the plaque. (emphasis on *Paul*)
> I saw him *running* down the hallway. (emphasis on *him*)

Infinitives

An infinitive is a verb form, usually preceded by *to.* It can be used as a noun, an adjective, or an adverb.

NOUN: *To win first prize* is her goal.   (Answers the question What?)
ADJECTIVE: The agent *to see about your problem* is Mr. Brooks.
              (Answers the question Which agent?)
ADVERB: *To succeed at Gibbs*, you must work hard.
              (Answers the question Why?)

Infinitives have both tense and voice:

	Present	**Perfect**
Active	to see	to have seen
Passive	to be seen	to have been seen

The present expresses action that occurs at the same time as the main verb.

> We were glad *to speak with you yesterday.*
> She intends *to be present today.*
> They are eager *to attend* the meeting.

The perfect form expresses action that occurred before the action in the main verb.

> I am proud *to have been associated with this firm for so long.*
> The lawyer proved the witness *to have been mistaken.*

Without to.   The sign of the infinitive, the word *to*, is omitted in certain constructions and after certain verbs such as *dare, feel, hear, help, let, make, need, please, see, and watch.*

> I wanted to run and hide. (to hide)
> We didn't dare repeat that story. (to repeat)
> He helped her do the report. (to do)
> The machine does everything but talk. (to talk)
> Please sign and return the enclosed form. (to sign and to return)

Infinitive absolute phrases.   An infinitive absolute has a subject in the nominative case and is related to the sentence in content but not in structure.

> That work will cost $15,000, we *to pay* only one-third.

Split infinitive.   A split infinitive occurs when one or more adverbs separate *to* from the verb. Such a split can be awkward and prevent the adverb(s) from functioning most effectively.

In general, split an infinitive only when doing so will improve readability.

> I decided not to take that course.
> We need to discuss your raise privately. (not *to privately discuss*)
> We plan to finish promptly at 4 PM. (not *to promptly finish*)

> We need *to really work* at finding a solution.
> It was a mistake *to even consider* their proposal.
> We hope *to more than triple* our profits next year.

Dangling Constructions

An introductory verbal phrase, an elliptical clause (one in which words are intentionally omitted), or a prepositional phrase beginning with *as* must logically describe the subject of the following clause; otherwise, the construction will dangle. To correct a dangling construction, make the subject of the clause the performer (or doer) of the action expressed in the verbal phrase. If that is not possible, reword the sentence.

DANGLING: *To succeed at Gibbs,* hard work is necessary.
(Hard work can't succeed at Gibbs.)
CORRECT: *To succeed at Gibbs,* you must work hard.

DANGLING: *By studying hard,* the test was easy to pass.
(The test can't study.)
CORRECT: *By studying hard,* the student passed the test easily.

DANGLING: *In analyzing these figures,* several errors were found.
(The errors can't analyze figures.)
CORRECT: *In analyzing these figures,* the auditor found several errors.

DANGLING: *When ordered before June 1,* 10 percent of the price will be dicounted. (Ten percent can't order before June 1.)
CORRECT: *When ordered before June 1,* the goods will be discounted by 10 percent.

DANGLING: *As the head of the committee,* we think you should speak at the convention. (*You* are the head of the committee, not *we.*)
CORRECT: We think that *as the head of the committee,* you should speak at the convention.

When verbal phrases and elliptical clauses are not introductory, be careful of illogical or confusing placement.

DANGLING: The dog grabbed the bone *running across the street.*
(The bone isn't running across the street.)
CORRECT: *Running across the street,* the dog grabbed the bone.

DANGLING: I saw three cars get into an accident *while running for the train.*
(The accident isn't running for the train.)
CORRECT: *While running for the train,* I saw three cars get into an accident.

Parts of Speech

Plurals and Possessives

CHAPTER 5 # Plurals and Possessives

105

Plurals

English has been enriched by words borrowed from peoples all over the world. Although the roots of most English words are found in Latin and German, French, American Indian, Eskimo, Spanish, and many other tongues have contributed to modern English. For this reason spelling is especially difficult, since some words—for example, those originating in Latin—have retained their Latin plurals, whereas others have adopted English plurals. You should always consult a reliable, preferably desk-sized dictionary when in doubt about a plural spelling.

Computerized spell-check is, of course, helpful. But spell-check doesn't recognize every variation and often labels correct words as wrong . Study the following rules for forming plurals to increase your speed and accuracy and to save yourself considerable time.

Two basic rules govern the formation of most English plurals:

Most nouns form the plural by adding s to the singular		**Nouns ending in s, x, ch, sh, or z** form the plural by adding **es** to the singular	
machine	machines	bus	buses
friend	friends	business	businesses
car	cars	fox	foxes
book	books	wish	wishes
quota	quotas	topaz	topazes
computer	computers	church	churches
alibi	alibis	lens	lenses
game	games	summons	summonses

Using the dictionary: When a noun forms its plural according to the two basic rules given above, the dictionary does <u>not</u> show the plural. In many dictionaries irregular plurals or those that may give trouble are shown. They are shortened where possible to save space and are syllabified where necessary.

EXAMPLES: **cit·y n.,** *pl.* **cit·ies**   **a·moe·ba n.,** *pl.* -**bas** or -**bae**
  bo·le·ro n., *pl.* -**ros**   **son-in-law n.,** *pl.* **sons-in-law**
  tooth n., *pl.* **teeth**

If an irregular plural is so different in spelling that it would appear far from the singular, it is entered additionally at its proper alphabetical place.
  lice n. *pl. of* louse

Note that in some dictionaries if two spellings are given connected by the word *or* or by a comma, both are considered acceptable. If two spellings are given connected by the word *also,* the first spelling is preferred.

Nouns ending with y

If a noun ends in **y preceded by a vowel**, add s to the singular.		If a noun ends in **y preceded by a consonant**, change the **y to i** and add **es** to the singular.	
boy	boys	lady	ladies
key	keys	reply	replies
alloy	alloys	copy	copies
delay	delays	liability	liabilities
attorney	attorneys	policy	policies

Nouns ending in o

If a noun ends in **o preceded by a vowel** or is a **musical term**, add **s** to the singular.

radio	radios
stereo	stereos
alto	altos
ratio	ratios

Usually If a noun ends in **o preceded by a consonant**, add **es** to the singular.

hero	heroes
potato	potatoes
tomato	tomatoes
cargo	cargoes *or* cargos
volcano	volcanoes *or* volcanos
but	
silo	silos
auto	autos

Nouns ending in f or fe

Most nouns ending in **f** or **fe** form the plural by adding **s** to the singular.

belief	beliefs
proof	proofs
safe	safes
tariff	tariffs

Some nouns ending in **f** or **fe**, form the the plural by changing the **f** or **fe** to **v** and adding **es** to the singular.

half	halves
life	lives
knife	knives
leaf	leaves

Nouns that change their spelling

Some irregular nouns form their plurals by **changing their internal spelling**.

foot	feet
woman	women
man	men
tooth	teeth
goose	geese
louse	lice
mouse	mice

Some irregular nouns form their plurals by adding **ren** or **en** to the singular.

child	children
ox	oxen

Some irregular nouns spell the singular and the plural the **same** way.

sheep	fish (*or* fishes)
species	salmon
deer	series
means	

Compound Nouns

A compound noun written as **one word** forms the plural by pluralizing the **final word** as if it stood alone.

wineglass	wineglasses
hatbox	hatboxes
cupful	cupfuls
railroad	railroads
drugstore	drugstores
tablespoon	tablespoons
daytime	daytimes
grandchild	grandchildren
strawberry	strawberries
bookshelf	bookshelves

EXCEPTION: passerby, passersby

A compound noun written as two or three **separate words**, with or without hyphens, forms the plural by pluralizing the **most important word**.

attorney at law	attorneys at law
editor in chief	editors in chief
runner-up	runners-up
stock exchange	stock exchanges
lieutenant general	lieutenant generals
senator-elect	senators-elect
letter of credit	letters of credit
account payable	accounts payable

Plurals and Possessives

When a compound does not contain a noun as one of its elements, pluralize the **final word**.

hang-up	hang-ups
showoff	showoffs
has-been	has-beens
tie-in	tie-ins
go-between	go-betweens
makeup	makeups

Some of these compounds have **two plural forms**.

court-martial	courts-martial
	court-martials
notary public	notaries public
	notary publics
attorney general	attorneys general
	attorney generals

Proper Nouns

Proper nouns ending in **s, x, z, sh**, and **ch** form the plural by adding **es** to the singular.

Other proper nouns including those or ending in **y** are made plural by adding **s** to the singular.

Surnames

Mr. Adams	the Adamses
Ms. Hendrix	the Hendrixes
Mrs. Van Ness	the Van Nesses
Mary March	the Marches
Helen Marsh	the Marshes
Eric Katz	the Katzes
Dr. James	the Jameses
Ms. Jones	the Joneses

Mr. Bell	the Bells
Mrs. Russo	the Russos
Mr. Ryder	the Ryders
Ruby Hall	the Halls
Jonas Salk	the Salks
Mr. Wolf	the Wolfs
Mr. Martino	the Martinos
Dr. Brody	the Brodys

First Names

Gladys	Gladyses
Tess	Tesses
Lois	Loises

Mary	Marys
Joe	Joes
Timothy	Timothys

Other Proper Nouns

| March | Marches |
| Monday | Mondays |

| Swede | Swedes |
| North Dakota | the Dakotas |

EXCEPTIONS: the Rockies, the Alleghenies, Februaries.

Nouns ending in s

Most nouns ending in **s** follow the basic rule of adding **es** (boss—bosses). There are some exceptions:

Some nouns ending in **s** are **always singular** and have no plural form.

> news
> happiness
>
> The news is good.

Some nouns ending in **s** are **always plural** and have no singular form.

trousers	thanks
savings	remains
winnings	goods
proceeds	earnings

Her savings are insured.

A few nouns ending in s are **either singular or plural**, depending on the context .

One means of transportation is...   *Several means* of transportation are...
A series of plays is being offered.   *Many* television *series* lose their popularity.
This species of duck is near extinction.   *Several species* of ducks are on this lake.

Nouns ending in ics

A noun ending in **ics** is **singular** when it names a science, a branch of learning, a course of study.

A noun ending in **ics** is **plural** when it names an activity or a quality or when it is used in a nonacademic sense.

Physics is an exact science.
Economics is a large field of study.
Statistics is a difficult course.

The *statistics* were overwhelming.
Athletics are performed in the gym
The *acoustics* of the hall are poor.

Personal Titles

Singular	Plural
Mr.	Messrs.
Mrs.	Mmes.
Miss	Misses
Ms.	Mss.
Dr.	Drs.

Plural titles are normally used only in very formal situations, such as on wedding invitations or in diplomatic documents. In ordinary usage retain the singular form and repeat it with each name.

Formal Usage
Messrs. Hunt and Hall
Mmes. White and Gore
Misses Playo and Cortez
Mss. Cohen and Conroy
Drs. Holmes and Mallory

Ordinary Usage
Mr. Hunt and Mr. Hall
Mrs. White and Mrs. Gore
Miss Playo and Miss Cortez
Ms. Cohen and Ms. Conroy
Dr. Holmes and Dr. Mallory

When a personal title applies to two people with the same surname, you may pluralize only the title (formal usage) or only the surname (ordinary usage).

Formal Usage
the Messrs. Herrold
the Misses Mallory
the Mmes. Holland
the Mss. McCarthy

Ordinary Usage
the Mr. Herrolds
the Miss Mallorys
the Mrs. Hollands
the Ms. McCarthys

Foreign Nouns

Some nouns adopted directly from a foreign language retain their original plural spelling. Some have been given English plurals. Some have two acceptable plural spellings, one English and one the original. Always check the dictionary to determine the correct spelling and to see whether one is preferred.

The following examples of such words, mostly Latin in origin, have been grouped according to the word ending, since that is what determines the formation of the plural.

	Singular	English Plural	Foreign Plural
Words Ending in us	alumnus		alumni
	apparatus	apparatuses or apparatus	
	focus	focuses	foci
	nucleus	nucleuses	nuclei
	radius	radiuses	radii
	status	statuses	
	stimulus		stimuli
Words Ending in a	agenda	agendas	
	alumna		alumnae
	antenna	antennas	antennae
	formula	formulas	formulae
	vertebra	vertebras	vertebrae
Words Ending in um	bacterium		bacteria
	curriculum	curriculums	curricula
	datum	datums	data
	medium	mediums	media
	memorandum	memorandums	memoranda
	referendum	referendums	referenda
	stratum	stratums	strata
	symposium	symposiums	symposia
Words Ending in o	graffito		graffiti
	virtuoso	virtuosos	virtuosi
Words Ending in on	automaton	automatons	automata
	criterion	criterions	criteria
	phenomenon	phenomenons	phenomena
Words Ending in ix or ex	appendix	appendixes	appendices
	index	indexes	indices
	vertex	vertexes	vertices
Words Ending in sis	analysis	analyses	
	basis	bases	
	crisis	crises	
	emphasis	emphases	
	parenthesis	parentheses	

NOTE: These are just a few examples. All words ending in **sis** form the plural by changing to **ses**.

Words Ending in eau	bureau	bureaus	bureaux
	plateau	plateaus	plateaux
	tableau	tableaus	tableaux

Abbreviations

(See chapter on Abbreviations for discussion of when to use them.)

Most **abbreviations** form the plural by adding **s** to the singular

No.	Nos.	CEO	CEOs
Dr.	Drs.	PTA	PTAs
Bro.	Bros.	M.D.	M.D.s
bldg.	bldgs.	IQ	IQs
dept.	depts.	Ph.D.	Ph.D.s

The abbreviations of most **weights and measures** are the same in the singular and the plural and are usually written without periods.

ounce (s)	oz	mile (s)	mi
foot (feet)	ft	degree (s)	deg
inch (es)	in	kilometer (s)	km
milliliter	ml	pound (s)	lb
yard (s)	yd	quart (s)	qt

The plurals of a few **single-letter abbreviations** consist of the same letter doubled.

p., pp.	(page, pages)	p. 42; pp. 42-48
f., ff.	(following page, lines, and so forth)	p. 247 f. ; p. 247 ff.
l., ll.	(line, lines)	l. 23; ll. 23-24

Letters

With **capital** letters add **s** to form the plural. Occasionally **'s** is added to the plural to avoid misreading. With **lowercase** letters use **'s** to form plural.

four Bs and three Cs on her report	Mind your p's and q's.
five A's on his report card but two U's	Cross your t's and dot your i's.
Your résumé contains too many I's.	

Words Used as Words

With **words used as words** add **s** to form the plural. Italicize the word. If italics are unavailable, underscore.

No *ifs*, *ands*, or *buts*.

Form the plural of a contraction by adding **s**.

don'ts	ma'ams
do's and don'ts	

Numbers

To form the plurals of **numbers in figures**, add **s**; **'s** is acceptable but not necessary.

Numbers expressed **in words** follow the basic rules

the 1960s	1960's	ones
the 1800s	1800's	twos
in his 50s	his 50's	sixes

Possessives

Possessive nouns are used to indicate ownership or possession. A possessive noun always ends in the sound of *s* and is formed with an apostrophe alone or with an apostrophe plus *s*. To be sure that the possessive form should be used, try substituting a prepositional phrase starting with *of, by,* or *belonging to*. If the substitution works, the possessive is needed.

> the company's headquarters (the headquarters of the company)
> my boss's office (the office of my boss)
> Mr. Wilson's report (the report of Mr. Wilson)
> Hemingway's *A Farewell to Arms* (*A Farewell to Arms* by Hemingway)
> my parents' home (the home of my parents)
> Joan's book (the book belonging to Joan)

Do not confuse an adjective ending in *s* with a possessive noun.

> a sales report   a savings account   a news item

In these three phrases *sales, savings,* and *news* function as adjectives.

Singular Possessives

Regardless of the last letter of the noun, most singular nouns are made possessive by adding an apostrophe and an *s* (*'s*).

> the student's schedule   the witness's story
> Roger's car   Charles's car
> the lawyer's advice   the child's toy
> my sister-in-law's son   the editor in chief's decision
> Dr. John Marcus Jr.'s office   Roger Thornton II's inheritance

If a singular noun ends in *s* and the resulting possessive form would sound awkward and be hard to pronounce, you may add just an apostrophe. Often, however, a new syllable is formed by the addition of the possessive, in which case you should always add the apostrophe plus *s*.

> Mr. Cousins' car   Mrs. Papadopulos' house   Mr. Perkins' restaurant

but

> the witness's statement   John Lopez's proposal
> John Harris's new house   Thomas's last name
> Congress's next session   Mr. and Mrs. Troulakis's garden
> Dallas's new airport   Arkansas's state flower

Plural Possessives

All regular plural nouns end in *s*. (See Plurals, page 106.) To form the possessive of a regular plural, add an apostrophe <u>after</u> the *s*.

> the nurses' uniforms   three students' reports
> attorneys' efforts   accountants' papers
> the agencies' offices   the Thomases' legal residence

To form the possessive of an irregular plural—that is, one that does not end in *s* (see Plurals, page 106)—add an apostrophe plus *s*.

the children's complaints	my sons-in-law's parents
the men's department	the editors in chief's meeting
the Women's Quilting Society	the alumni's registration forms

Because a singular possessive and a plural possessive often sound exactly alike, care must be taken when forming possessives.

Singular	Singular Poss. (add 's)	Plural	Plural Poss. (add ' after s; add 's after other letters)
a boy	a boy's bicycle	two boys	two boys' bicycles
my boss	my boss's office	our bosses	the bosses' time
one child	one child's friend	children	children's toys
Mr. Bell	Mr. Bell's house	the Bells	the Bells' house
brother-in-law	my brother-in-law's car	brothers-in-law	my brothers-in-law's cars
a man	a man's necktie	men	men's neckties
a woman	a woman's blouse	women	women's dresses

Joint and Separate Possession

Joint Possession

When two or more people share ownership or possession, add 's after the <u>last</u> individual name.

Nancy and Tom's store
Ms. Oliver and Ms. Adams's shop
Mr. and Mrs. Cortinez's cars

Separate Possession

When ownership or possession is separate, add 's after <u>each</u> name.

the buyer's and seller's signatures.
men's and children's clothes
Alice's and her husband Joe's parents

Organization and Publication Names

Always follow the preference of a company or publication for the spelling of its name. (You'll find it helpful to check the letterhead or make a telephone call.) You will find, however, that most company or publication names containing a <u>regular plural</u>—that is, a plural ending in *s*—do not use the apostrophe. If the name contains a singular possessive, the apostrophe plus *s* is always used.

Reader's Digest (SINGULAR)
Consumers Digest (REGULAR PLURAL)
Ladies' Home Journal (COMPANY PREFERENCE)
Munsey Park Women's Club (IRREGULAR PLURAL)
American Bankers Association (REGULAR PLURAL)

Other Possessives

As a rule, nouns referring to inanimate things should not be in the possessive. Use an *of phrase* instead.

the cover of the book *or* the book cover (not the book's cover)
the upper floor of the building (not the building's upper floor)
the bottom of the barrel (not the barrel's bottom)

However, certain expressions dealing with time and value, as well as other idiomatic expressions are written in the possessive form.

Time	Value	Distance
one day's notice	a dollar's worth	at arm's length
an hour's work	several dollars' worth	a stone's throw
two years' growth	10 cents' worth	
a moment's delay	Ten dollars' worth	
this morning's news	your money's worth	

Idiomatic Expressions

the sun's rays	New Year's resolutions	the water's edge
for conscience' sake	the earth's atmosphere	Saturn's climate
a baker's dozen	seller's market	a collector's item

Possessives Preceding Gerunds

A gerund is the *ing* form of a verb used as a noun (see page 99). The subject of a gerund, therefore, should be in the possessive case.

> I should appreciate *your letting* me know by Tuesday.
> (your—POSSESSIVE; *letting* is A GERUND)

> The *children's dancing* was charming.
> (children's—POSSESSIVE; *dancing* is A GERUND)

> There is no point in *Mr. Hall's refusing* to cooperate.
> (Mr. Hall's—POSSESSIVE; *refusing* is A GERUND)

Possessives in Elliptical Constructions

When the object possessed is not expressed but is clearly understood, show possession just the same as if the word were there.

> His average is as good as his sister's. (meaning his sister's average)
> You will have a week's vacation this year and two weeks' next year.
> (meaning two weeks' vacation)

Possessive Pronouns

The possessive forms of the personal pronouns and of the pronoun *who* <u>never</u> employ an apostrophe.

Personal Pronoun	Possessive
I	my, mine
you	your, yours
he	his
she	her, hers
it	its (<u>never</u> its')
we	our, ours
they	their, theirs
who	whose

Mary has been a friend of *hers* for years. (<u>never</u> *her's*)
Each gift comes in *its* own specially designed box. (<u>never</u> *its'*)

Be especially careful not to confuse the possessive *its* with the contraction *it's*, meaning *it is*.

> *It's* (it is) time to give the dog *its* dinner.

Indefinite Pronouns

Many indefinite pronouns have possessive forms. Only *others* can be plural—*others'*.

another's	anybody's	anyone's	anyone else's
each one's	each other's	either one's	everyone's
neither one's	no one's	one another's	one's
somebody's	someone's	someone else's	other's (singular)
			others' (plural)

> *Someone's* glasses were left on the table.
> *No one's* résumé was considered acceptable.
> I can't find my papers nor *anyone else's*.
> The *others'* opinions were not taken into consideration.

Abbreviations

An abbreviation is treated the same way as any noun when forming the possessive.

> the FCC's ruling   the CPA's report   the CPAs' meeting

Appositives

Sometimes a noun that ordinarily would be in the possessive is followed by an appositive (a noun that renames and explains the preceding noun). In such cases the appositive is made possessive.

> Mr. Wilson, my manager's, request.
> Mary, my friend's, apartment.

Possessives in Holidays

Note the spellings of the following holidays:

Mother's Day   New Year's Eve
Lincoln's Birthday   Valentine's Day
Presidents' Day   St. Patrick's Day
Veterans Day   April Fools' Day
Columbus Day

Proper Adjectives

You can choose to use a singular proper noun as an adjective preceded by the word *the* to express the concept of ownership. Do not then use an apostrophe.

Proper Adjective	**Possessive**
the Burns home	the Burnses' home
the Nixon tapes	Richard Nixon's tapes
the California climate	California's climate
the Harris estate	the Harrises' estate

You can choose to use a compound adjective (usually hyphenated) to express concepts of time and value. Do not use an apostrophe in these constructions.

a *six-month* leave	**or**	*six months'* leave of absence
a *one-mile* hike		*15 days'* grace period
a *10-cent* reduction		
a *15-day* grace period		

CHAPTER 6 # Compound Words

Compound Words

Compound Words

A compound word may be formed by combining two or more independent words or by adding a prefix or suffix to an independent word. Compound words may be written as solids, as separate words, or as hyphenated words. Not only do some authorities disagree on several of these principles, but style is continually changing so that many combinations that used to be hyphenated are now written as solids or as separate words.

The spellings in this section, as in the rest of this text, are based on *Webster's New World Dictionary, Tenth Edition.* Other dictionaries will differ in the spelling of compounds. The following rules give you some idea about the formation of compound words, but in no area of English are there more exceptions to the so-called rules. Thus, remember to consult your dictionary!

Using the Dictionary.   Compound words spelled with hyphens or spelled as solids are listed alphabetically in the dictionary just like any other word. Be sure to distinguish between a hyphen (-) and the center dot (·), which is generally used to show a break between syllables. Some but not all two-word compounds are listed. Other combinations such as noun + participle may have some representative examples but not every possibility. If a specific compound word is not listed, look for a comparable example and spell accordingly.

Compound Verbs

Compound verbs can be hyphenated or solid. Some examples:

air-condition	double-park	airdrop	shortchange
air-cool	dry-clean	bulldoze	spotlight
air-dry	short-circuit	downsize	mastermind
blue-pencil	spot-check	handpick	offload
double-space	spot-weld	highlight	proofread

Compound Nouns

Compound nouns follow no regular pattern. Even those that sound alike may be spelled in different ways. Always check your dictionary.

Closed	Open	Hyphenated
checklist	check mark	check-in
closeout	close shave	close-up
copyright	copy editor	
courtroom	court reporter	court-martial
crossroad	cross section	cross-reference
eyewitness	eye shadow	eye-opener
fullback	full moon	
halftone	half note	half-wit
moneylender	money order	money-changer
nightlight	night court	
salesroom	sales tax	
salesclerk	sales representative	
trademark	trade wind	trade-in

	Closed	**Hyphenated**
Up Words	checkup hookup makeup setup	mix-up runner-up shake-up write-up
Down Words	countdown markdown	put-down sit-down
In Words		break-in stand-in tie-in
Out Words	layout sellout workout	fade-out falling-out
On Words		come-on goings-on put-on
Off Words	playoff showoff spinoff	sell-off trade-off write-off
Over Words	stopover turnover	going-over once-over
Back Words	setback tieback	
Away Words	layaway stowaway	
Miscellaneous	breakthrough passersby runaround	go-between follow-through

Many of these compound nouns resemble common idiomatic combinations, which are never hyphenated.

> She will have to *make up* the test on Thursday.
> You must *follow up* on the details.
> He will *go ahead* with the proposal.
> Let's *run through* the contingency plan once again.
> We plan to *get together* for the holidays.

Hyphenate a compound noun formed from other parts of speech.

> cure-all   go-getter   has-been   look-alike   give-and-take

Compound nouns that end with a prepositional phrase are often but not always written as separate words. Most of these were formerly hyphenated.

> attorney at law   line of credit   brother-in-law
> bill of lading   power of attorney   father-in-law
> editor in chief   right of way   theater-in-the-round
> chief of staff   commander in chief   ambassador-at-large

Hyphenate a compound signifying that a person has two equal functions.

actor-director   clerk-typist   secretary-treasurer

Do not hyphenate civil, military, and naval titles of two or more words.

General Manager Smith   Attorney General Hernandez
Rear Admiral Johnstone   Chief of Police Brown

Most compound nouns with a letter as the first element are hyphenated.

T-shirt   X-ray   T-bill   D-major   **but**   T square

Compound Adjectives

Perhaps in no other area of the language do we see as much creativity and bending of the rules as in our formation of compound adjectives. New words are continually being created to express new information in ever more vivid and descriptive ways. The majority of compound words are adjectives, and the main way we get those words is by combining two other words, often two parts of speech that don't belong together according to traditional rules of grammar.

These coined words are frequently hyphenated when they first come into use; many later become solid words. Combined elements that carry a hyphen are <u>always</u> hyphenated before the noun. The current trend is to drop the hyphen when the compound is used as a predicate adjective, except when misreading would result. Study the following combinations of words hyphenated to serve as adjectives. Some of these are found in the dictionary; some are not. If you don't find a particular word in your dictionary, hyphenate it if it fits one of the following patterns; otherwise, write it as two words.

Adjective + noun combinations are usually hyphenated before the noun but are left unhyphenated after the noun unless misreading is a problem.

high-energy	low-cost	full-scale	short-term
high-class	low-grade	full-length	part-time
high-grade	low-key	middle-class	full-time
highbrow	low-level	middleweight	lowland

Hyphenated	**Not Hyphenated**
a high-strung animal	The cat is high strung around children.
a low-cost alternative	The alternative is very low cost.
a middle-class family	That family is middle class.

Adjective + noun + ed combinations are usually hyphenated.

coarse-grained	able-bodied	red-faced	tightfisted
straight-sided	close-lipped	time-tested	bighearted
broad-based	clear-sighted	good-natured	nearsighted
high-spirited	middle-aged	old-fashioned	bareheaded
open-minded	open-mouthed	left-handed	evenhanded

Compound Words

Adjective + participle combinations are usually hyphenated before a noun, not hyphenated as a predicate adjective, and not hyphenated if modified by another adverb. The adjective may be in the positive, comparative, or superlative degree.

long-playing	far-reaching	sweet-smelling	little-known
attractive-looking	even-numbered	ill-fitting	high-strung
ready-made	good-looking	far-flung	lesser-regarded
scholarly-appearing	soft-spoken	short-lived	full-fledged
better-prepared	best-dressed	little-understood	full-blown

Hyphenated	**Not hyphenated**
an ill-fitting suit	a very ill fitting suit
the better-prepared student	a much better prepared student
the best-dressed list	She is the best dressed student on campus.
a little-understood concept	The concept is little understood.
a lesser-regarded school	The school is somewhat lesser regarded.

Although *well*, as used here, is an adverb, **well + participle** follows this same practice.

well-known	well-acted	well-prepared
well-thought-out	well-bred	well-meaning

Hyphenated	**Not Hyphenated**
a well-known author	the author is well known.
a well-acted play	the play was well acted.
a well-prepared speech	a very well prepared speech
a well-thought-out program	a very well accepted program

If a well word cannot be reversed smoothly, it should be hyphenated even when functioning as a predicate adjective.

a well-advised plan	the plan is well-advised
a well-bred young woman	the young woman is well-bred
a well-meaning remark	the remark is well-meaning
the well-worn teddy bear	the teddy bear is well-worn

Be sure to distinguish between an adjective that ends in *ly* (noun + *ly* = ADJECTIVE) and an adverb that ends in *ly* (adjective + *ly* = ADVERB). The adjective is hyphenated when joined to a participle; the adverb is not.

Adjective + Participle	**Adverb + Participle**
a neighborly-seeming person	a widely known fact
a friendly-looking young woman	a beautifully arranged bouquet
	highly developed species
	poorly dressed applicant

Noun + participle combinations are usually hyphenated in all adjective positions.

air-cooled	government-owned	price-cutting	handmade
awe-inspiring	machine-made	profit-sharing	moneymaking
decision-making	grief-stricken	time-consuming	timesaving
dust-covered	panic-stricken	thought-provoking	bookkeeping
duty-free	motor-driven	interest-bearing	dressmaking

Do not hyphenate these combinations when they are used as nouns.

Hyphenated	**Not hyphenated**
a profit-sharing plan	He participates in profit sharing.
an air-conditioning unit	She installed air conditioning.
their price-cutting policy	They specialize in price cutting.

Noun + adjective combinations are hyphenated in all adjective positions.

labor-intensive	fuel-efficient	user-friendly
paper-thin	cost-effective	capital-intensive
tax-exempt	tax-free	cross-cultural

Participle + adverb combinations are hyphenated before a noun but not elsewhere.

tuned-up	worn-out	filled-in	built-in
unheard-of	cooling-off	spelled-out	

Two or more colors of equal weight are hyphenated when used as a compound adjective. Other modifiers are not hyphenated.

blue-green dress	red-orange crayon	pale pink lipstick
bluish green eyes	black-and-white photos	coal black hair

Two or more separate proper nouns or adjectives are hyphenated as a compound adjective.

the New York-Washington shuttle	British-French talks
the Minneapolis-St. Paul area	Scottish-Irish descent

A compound proper noun is not hyphenated as an adjective modifier.

Fifth Avenue shops	a Supreme Court decision
the 42d Street entrance	Legal Department personnel

Foreign words and phrases are not hyphenated when used as compound modifiers.

à la carte luncheon	ex officio member
bon voyage gift	per diem employee
bona fide offer	prima facie evidence

Letter + noun or participle combinations are hyphenated as a one-thought modifier before a noun.

X-ray treatment	L-shaped living room

Adjectival phrases are hyphenated when used before a noun. Some are hyphenated after a noun; others are not.

over-the-counter medicine	The medicine was sold over the counter.
ready-to-wear fashions	This garment is ready to wear.
up-to-standard work	Our work is up to standard.
out-of-state taxpayers	She works out of state.
house-to-house survey	He canvassed from house to house.

easy-to-understand directions	The directions are easy to understand.
a matter-of-fact attitude	His attitude is matter-of-fact.
an up-to-date report	The report was up-to-date.
an over-the-hill centerfielder	The centerfielder was over the hill.
lighter-than-air pastry	Good pastry is lighter than air.
better-than-average results	The results are better than average.
a down-payment plan	Tom made a down payment.
a long-past-due account	Their account is long past due.
an under-the-table payment	Payments made under the table are illegal.

Numbers

Hyphenate spelled-out numbers consisting of two words between 21 and 99.

> She now is twenty-three.
> Ninety-nine students are in the graduating class.
> A check for seven hundred fifty-six dollars ($756) was cashed by John Smith.

Hyphenate spelled-out fractions used as adjectives, adverbs, or nouns.

two-thirds majority	The roast is three-fourths done.
one-half percent	One-half of the participants succeeded.

Hyphenate a number-word combination used as a one-thought adjective before a noun it modifies. When these expressions are used elsewhere in a sentence, they are not hyphenated. Note: In a hyphenated combination, the unit of measurement is always singular even with a plural number. In an unhyphenated combination, the number and the unit of measurement agree —that is, both singular or both plural.

Hyphenated	Not Hyphenated
a one-story building	a building one story high
a six-year term	a term of six years
a 50-cent raise	a raise of fifty cents
an 8-foot ceiling	a ceiling of 8 feet
the first-floor apartment	an apartment on the first floor
an early 20th-century poet	a poet of the early 20th century

Other words may be added to the basic unit with hyphens.

24-hour-a-day service	service 24 hours a day
a two-year-old boy	a boy two years old
a 10-inch-thick panel	a panel 10 inches thick.
a 50-foot-wide trench	a trench 50 feet wide

When the base word is expressed only once, a hyphen and a space—called a *suspended hyphen*—follow all but the last member of the compound.

a 9- by 12-foot room	a room 9 by 12 feet
6-, 8-, and 10-minute intervals	intervals of 6, 8, and 10 minutes

Hyphenate a sum of money joined to other words to form a one-thought modifier before the noun but not elsewhere in the sentence.

Hyphenated	Not Hyphenated
a $50-a-week raise	a raise of $50 a week
a $150-a-day per diem	a per diem of $150 a day

Hyphenate compound adjectives combining a number and the words *odd* or *plus*.

The scandal occurred *twenty-odd* years ago.
I guessed his age to be *forty-plus*.

Hyphenate compound adjectives involving two numbers, as in ratios and scores.

a 50-50 chance   a 28-27 victory   a 100-to-1 chance

Prefixes and Suffixes

Nearly all compound words formed with prefixes and suffixes are written as solids, whether they are used as adjectives, adverbs, nouns, or verbs.

anteroom	harmful	nonessential	reorganize
antihero	homestead	nonnegotiable	retroactive
backward	hyperactive	offroad	sadness
biosphere	illegal	outrun	sixfold
biweekly	immaterial	overconfident	socioeconomic
booklet	infrastructure	paramedic	subdivide
byline	interoffice	parsonage	supernatural
censorship	intramural	photograph	thankless
changeable	introversion	polysyllable	topmost
childlike	macroeconomics	postpartum	transcontinental
coauthor	microprocessor	preempt	trustworthy
coordinate	midlife	prerequisite	ultraliberal
counterbalance	minibike	proponent	underage
decentralize	misspell	prototype	uninformed
edgewise	monosyllable	pseudoscientific	uphold
forefront	multifaceted	reexamine	waterproof
fortyish	nationwide	refinement	winsome
freedom	neonatal		

EXCEPTIONS:
Use a hyphen to add a prefix to a proper noun or a number.

anti-Arab	mid-1986	post-World War II	pre-Civil War
mid-August	mid-sixties	non-English-speaking	

However: transatlantic, transpacific, the Midwest, the Mideast

Use a hyphen to distinguish two words that sound alike but have different meanings (homographs). Check your dictionary because these are not consistent.

Hyphenated	Not Hyphenated
re-cover the couch with new fabric	*recover* the stolen money
a *re-creation* of the Battle of Gettysburg	*recreation* facility
he needs to *re-lay* the tile.	Please *relay* a message to her.
a *co-op* board	a chicken *coop*
please *re-collect* the cards	Please try to *recollect* the event.
They will *re-lease* the car.	He will *release* the figures.
	He *recounts* the tale with gusto, but the board will *recount* the votes.

Compound Words

Use a hyphen to prevent misreading when the prefix ends with an *a* or *i* and the base word starts with the same letter.

    anti-intellectual   semi-independent   ultra-ambitious

The majority of words prefixed by *co* are solid, but there are exceptions:

    co-anchor   co-owner   co-opt   co-worker

Use a hyphen when *self* is the prefix.

    self-addressed   self-confidence   self-supporting
    self-evident   self-effacing   self-indulgent

      but   unselfconscious

Omit the hyphen when *self* is the base word and a suffix is added.

    selfish   selfless   selfhood   selfsame

The prefixes *all*, *cross*, *full,* and *half* are usually hyphenated.

    all-inclusive   all-around   all-out
    all-important   all-purpose   all-star

      but   allover

    cross-reference   cross-country   cross-grain

      but   crossbred
             crosscut

    full-length   full-blown   full-scale

      but   fullback

    half-baked   half-length   half-life

      but   halfway
             halfhearted

Hyphenate family terms involving the prefix *great* or the suffix *in-law*, but terms involving *step* and *grand* are solid.

    great-grandfather   grandmother   brother-in-law
    great-aunt   grandson   stepdaughter

Use a hyphen to join *ex* and *elect* to titles and to common nouns. *Former* is not hyphenated.

    ex-premier   President-elect Hayes   the former mayor
    ex-wife   ex-President Mayo   my former employer

      but   ex officio
             ex libris

Many but not all *vice* titles are hyphenated.

Vice-Chairman Spenser   Vice-President Black   Vice Admiral Cox

NOTE: Vice President of the United States is typically not hyphenated.

See the Glossary of Usage, page 132, for compound words that are sometimes one word, sometimes two.

End-of-Line Word Division

Word processors typically do not hyphenate at the end of a typed line. This practice, however, can lead to very irregular righthand margins. You should, therefore, divide words at the end of the line when you want to save space and make your margin more even. Using a word processor to right-justify may lead to irregular spacing within the paragraph and make reading comprehension more difficult.

Follow these editorial rules to syllabify words at the end of a line.

Do not divide a word at the end of the first line of typing, at the end of a paragraph, or at the end of a page.

Do not end more than two consecutive lines with a hyphen.

Consult your dictionary and divide only between syllables.

Do not divide a word of one syllable.

length   styles   through

Divide a hyphenated word only at the hyphen.

by-product   self-respect

Keep the suffixes *able, ible,* and *uble* intact.

advis-able   revers-ible   vol-uble

Divide compound words into their separate elements.

business-men   every-where

Follow the 3-3 rule—that is, be sure you have at least three characters (not letters) at the end of a line when you divide.

enough   about   copy   abso-lutely

Divide after a syllable of one letter, unless doing so would violate the 3-3 rule.

competi-tor   holi-day   read-ily

Divide between two single-letter syllables.

perpetu-ator   medi-ation   perpetu-ity

Special Cases

Names and Titles   If a person's name or title must be divided,

Keep the first name or initials on the same line with the courtesy title.

> . . .for the purpose of welcoming the director, Ms. J. C.
> Martinson, the committee. . .

You may divide a long title of respect or position from the name.

> . . . received a cordial invitation from the Honorable
> Jonathan B. Woodbridge of. . .

Do not divide Jr., Sr., and Esq. from the rest of the name.

Addresses   If a street name has two or more words, separate between two words.

> She moved last month to 15 Pelham
> Manor Road.

You may divide such words as Street, Avenue, and Road from the rest of the street address in the body of a letter.

> He said that they preferred the office at Nine Center
> Street.

Divide place names between the city and the state or between the state and the ZIP Code.

> Chicago,   Brooklyn, New York
> Illinois   11209-2053

You may divide between the two words of a state name.

> New   South
> Jersey   Carolina

You may divide long state names when necessary.

> Cali-fornia   Califor-nia

Dates   You may divide between a day and year. Do not hyphenate.

> The last check you sent us was dated April 8,
> 1995.

Telephone numbers   Divide between the area code and the rest of the number.

> Area Code 212
> 555-7576

Abbreviations   Do not divide abbreviations or short numbers from the elements they belong to.

> COD   No. 43   Style 980   4 PM

CHAPTER 7 **Glossary of Usage**

CHAPTER 7 Glossary of Usage

a, an
about, at
accept, except
adapt, adept, adopt
adverse, averse
advice, advise, inform
affect, effect
aggravate, irritate
a lot, alot, allot
all of
all ready, already
all right, alright
all together
   altogether
always, all ways
allusion, illusion
almost, most
although, whereas,
   while
alumna, alumnae
alumnus, alumni
among, between
amount, number
and etc.
anxious, eager

anymore, any more
anyone, any one
anyplace
any time
any way, anyway
anywhere, anywheres
apiece, a piece
appraise, apprise
apt to, liable to, likely to
as, like
ascent, assent
assure, ensure, insure
awhile, a while
bad, badly
balance
because of, due to
being as, being that
beside, besides
be sure and, to be sure
biannual, biennial, semiannual
   bimonthly, semimonthly
both
bring, take
but...however
can, could, may, might

cannot
can't hardly, can't scarcely
can't help but
capital, capitol, Capitol
cite, sight, site
come, go
compare, contrast
complement, compliment(s)
consensus
consul, council, counsel
continually, continuously
could have, could of
credible, creditable
data
descend, descent, dissent
different, differently
different from, different than
disburse, disperse
disinterested, uninterested
done, don't
double negatives
each other, one another
elicit, illicit
emigrate, immigrate
eminent, imminent

envelop, envelope
equally as
etc.
everyday, every day
everyone, every one
farther, further
fewer, less, lesser
first
foreword, forward
formally, formerly
former, latter
good, well
got, have got to
healthful, healthy
hopefully
if, whether
imply, infer
ingenious, ingenuous
in, in to, into
in regards to
irregardless
it, there
its, it's
kind of, sort of, type of
late, last, latest

lay, lie
lead, led
leave, let
lend, loan
lose, loose
ly adverbs
makeup, make up
may, might
maybe, may be
meantime
media
more important,
    more importantly
nobody, no body
off
paid, payed
passed, past
per, a
personal, personnel
precede, proceed
principal, principle
prior to
proved, proven
provided, providing
quiet, quite

raise, rise
real, really, sure, surely
reason is that
recommend, refer
respectfully, respectively
said
same
serve, service
set, sit
shall, should, will, would
so, so that
somday, some day
sometime
sometime, sometimes
stationary, stationery
than, then
that, which
their, there, they're
theirs, there's
up
way, ways
weather, whether
who's, whose
you're, your

Glossary of Usage

Standard English usage is based on the language of educated speakers and writers. Usage, however, is constantly changing. Expressions now unacceptable may become standard. Usage formerly criticized is now accepted. A good modern dictionary is therefore essential. This glossary was prepared using *Webster's New World Dictionary of American English, Third College Edition.*

Formal English is characterized by longer sentences, more difficult vocabulary, and few contractions. Modern written business English avoids both the stiffness of the very formal and the casualness of everyday conversation. Such writing should be clear and concise, reflecting careful and precise word choice.

Some of the following entries are labeled colloquial, which is defined as "characteristic of conversation and informal writing." Although such words may be perfectly acceptable in most conversation, avoid them in written business English.

The following list, which is not all-inclusive, is alphabetically arranged for easy reference. It contains words and expressions that are often misused and confused. If you need more detailed information or if you do not find the word you are seeking, consult your dictionary.

a, an
In choosing *a* or *an*, consider the sound, not the spelling, of the word that follows. Use *a* before a consonant sound, including long *u*, a sounded *h*, or an *o* pronounced like *w*. Examples: *a* broker, *a* wonderful invention, *a* unique experience (long *u* begins with the sound of *y* as in yellow), *a* handful (sounded *h*), *a* one-way street (begins with the sound of *w*, as in won).

Use *an* before a vowel sound: *an* appointment, *an* FOB (sounds like *ef*) shipment, *an* heir (silent *h*), *an* honor (silent *h*), *an* understanding.

about, at (prep)
Use one or the other, not both.
> I will meet you *about* 6:30. (approximate)
> I will meet you *at* 6:30. (precise)

accept, except
accept—(v) receive; take
> I readily *accept* the blame.
except—(v) omit or exclude.
> She *excepted* all late entries.
except—(prep) other than; but
> I will finish everything *except* the tasks assigned today.

adapt, adept, adopt
adapt—(v) change so as to make suitable.
> We *adapted* the building to our needs.
adept—(adj) skilled; expert
> She is *adept* at carpentry.
adopt—(v) take as one's own.
> The board *adopted* the committee's suggestion.

132

adverse, averse
adverse—(adj) unfavorable; harmful
>It is difficult to work under such *adverse* conditions.

averse—(adj) not willing; reluctant
>I am *averse* to continuing this discussion.

advice, advise, inform
advice—(n) opinion; counsel
>I would appreciate your *advice* on this matter.

advise—(v) recommend
>He *advised* me to reconsider my decision.

inform—(v) tell
>My lawyer *informed* me that parts of the contract are unclear.

affect, effect
affect—(v) influence; make a pretense of
>The weather *affects* his mood. She *affected* a sophisticated air.

effect—(v) bring about; produce
>The company is *effecting* many improvements.

effect—(n) consequence or result
>What *effect* did the recent strike have on morale?

effects—(n) property
>Their personal *effects* were given to charity.

aggravate, irritate
aggravate—(v) make worse
>He *aggravated* the problem by acting too quickly.

irritate—(v) excite to anger; provoke; annoy
>His boastful behavior never fails to *irritate* me.

a lot, alot, allot
a lot—(adj + noun) many; much
>He spends *a lot* of his time at the computer.

alot, an incorrect spelling for *a lot*, is never acceptable.

allot—(v) apportion
>He *allotted* three disks to each student.

all of
Do not use *of* unless a pronoun follows.
>*All* the committee members will be here.
>*All of* them signed the roster.

all ready, already
all ready—(pron + adj) completely prepared
>My staff was *all ready* for the meeting.

already—(adv) previously
>They have *already* completed the required work.

all right, alright
all right—(pron + adj) satisfactory; completely correct
>The answers she gave were *all right.*

alright , an incorrect spelling for *all right,* is never acceptable.

Glossary of Usage

all together, altogether

all together—(pron + adv) in a group; in one place

> We usually have our books *all together* before we start to work.
>
> *All together*, there were eleven of us.

altogether—(adv) entirely; on the whole

> It was *altogether* too warm for comfort.
>
> The project was completed *altogether* satisfactorily.

all ways, always

all ways—(adj + n) every manner or method

> I have examined *all ways* of solving this problem.

always—(adv) at all times

> She is *always* the first to arrive.
>
> *Always* be prepared for the worst.

allusion, illusion

allusion—(n) indirect reference

> His *allusion* to the board's recent proposal went unnoticed.

illusion—(n) an unreality

> The promise of increased profits proved to be just an *illusion*.

almost, most

almost—(adj) nearly

Use *almost*, not *most*, to modify *all, any, anybody, anyone, anything, everybody, everyone, everything, nobody, no one,* and *nothing.*

> We have called *almost* all the board members.
>
> *Almost* everyone was present at the meeting.
>
> INCORRECT: *Most* anyone can complete this course.

most—(adv) superlative form of *more*

Use before an adjective or adverb to mean to the highest degree only when more than two items are compared.

> Miss Williams is the *most* cordial of all the receptionists.
>
> The actors are seen *most* clearly from the expensive seats.
>
> It was the *most* unruly crowd I have ever seen.

most—(adj or pron) the majority

> *Most* letterheads are conservative in appearance.
>
> *Most* of the folders have been rechecked.

Do not use *most* as a modifier when no comparison is intended. Instead, use an adverb such as *greatly, very,* or *exceedingly.*

> Miss Wells was *very* cordial (not *most* cordial) to the visitors.
>
> He was *exceedingly* careful (not *most* careful) in all his work.

although, whereas, while

although—(conj)

Use *although* when the adverbial clause expresses concession.

> *Although* we have a sufficient supply of paper on hand, we intend to accept one more shipment.

whereas—(conj)

Use *whereas* when the adverbial clause expresses contrast.

> Iron rusts, *whereas* steel resists corrosion.

while—(conj) Use *while* when the adverbial clause expresses time.

> Mr. Croft will supervise the department *while* he is away.
>
> *While* I am sick, I will stay home from work.

alumnus, alumna, alumni, alumnae
alumnus—(n) male graduate; *alumni* is the plural
alumna—(n) female graduate; *alumnae* is the plural
Alumni also is used for male and female combined.
> She is an *alumna* of Barnard; he is an *alumnus* of Harvard.
> All *alumni* were notified of the upcoming reunion.

among, between
among—(prep)
Use when referring to more than two. Avoid using *amongst*.
> A heated discussion went on *among* the board members.
between—(prep)
Use when referring to two.
> The two of us discussed it *between* ourselves.
Between is used for more than two when each member of the group is relating individually to each of the others.
> The negotiations resulted in arms agreements *between* the three nations.

amount, number
amount—(n) refers to a singular word
> I was surprised at the *amount* of paperwork in that office.
number—(n) refers to a plural word
> The *number* of papers to review is staggering.

and etc.
And etc. is a redundant expression. *Etc.* is the abbreviation for the Latin phrase *et cetera*, meaning *and so forth*.
> Our inventory includes sewing notions: thread, zippers, buttons, interfacing, *etc.* (not *and etc.*)

anxious, eager
anxious—(adj) worried, uneasy
> She is *anxious* about the results of the difficult examination.
eager—(adj) enthusiastic
> We are *eager* to hear the details of your innovative proposal.

anymore, any more
anymore—(adv) nowadays, at present
> He doesn't work here *anymore.*
any more—(adv + adj) anything additional
> Do you have *any more* suggestions?

anyone, any one
anyone—(pron) one word when used alone to mean a person
> *Anyone* can do the job.
any one—(adj + pron) two words when used with an "of phrase" or to mean one thing
> *Any one* of the boys will help you.
> Which book do you want? Give me *any one.*

anyplace
—(adv) Colloquial for the word *anywhere.* Use *anywhere* in formal business correspondence.
> She is willing to travel *anywhere* the job requires.

Glossary of Usage

any time

—(adj + n) Always write as two words.

> Do you have *any time* to see me?

any way, anyway

any way—(adj + noun) by any method.

> I will help you in *any way* I can.

anyway—(adv) nevertheless

> He is busy but will attend the meeting *anyway*.

anywhere, anywheres

anywhere—(adv) Always write as one word.

> Put the package *anywhere* you can.

anywheres—(adv)

> Colloquial for *anywhere*. Do not use in business writing.

apiece, a piece

apiece—(adv) each

> The textbooks sell for $30 *apiece*.

a piece—(adj + n) a part of the whole

> He gave her *a piece* of cake.

appraise, apprise

appraise—(v) estimate; value

> The property was *appraised* at $300,000.

apprise—(v) inform

> She *apprised* him of her manager's resignation.

apt to, liable to, likely to

apt to—(adj) expresses habitual tendency

> She is *apt to* leave that job to her secretary.

liable to—(adj) expresses risk

> The pavement is icy, and the car is *liable to* skid.

likely to—(adj) expresses probability

> Their report is *likely to* be accepted quickly.

as

(conj) Do not confuse with *that* or *whether*.

> I do not know *whether* (not *as*) you will be invited.

Do not substitute *as* for the more exact and effective conjunctions *since, because,* and *when*.

> *Because* (not *as*) the weather was bad, we knew our train would be delayed.

as, like

as—(conj) in the same manner that

> She writes *as* she talks—bluntly.

as—(prep) in the function, role, or sense of

> *As* a supervisor, she is always fair.

like—(prep) similar to

> She sounds just *like* you on the phone.

Like should not be used as a conjunction—that is, followed by a subject and verb—in written business English.

COLLOQUIAL: Nobody works *like* she does.

CORRECT: Nobody works *as* she does.

Never use *like* as a substitute for *as if* or *as though*.

She acted *as if* (not *like*) she hadn't heard the news.

ascent, assent

ascent—(n) advancement, upward movement.

They made their *ascent* to the observation deck of the World Trade Center.

assent—(v) agree; (n) permission.

Did they *assent* to the board's recent proposal?

Mrs. Williams gave her *assent* to the changes.

assure, ensure, insure

assure—(v) cause to feel confidence

I *assure* you we can solve your problem.

ensure—(v) make certain or safe; protect

Careful proofreading *ensures* accuracy.

insure—(v) protect against risk or financial loss

We will *insure* all your new equipment.

at   See **about, at**.

averse   See **adverse, averse**.

awhile, a while

awhile—(adv) an unspecified amount of time

He has been gone *awhile*.

a while—(adj + n) an unspecified amount of time

Use in a prepositional phrase and with *ago*.

He has been gone for *a while*.

I saw him in the conference room just *a while* ago.

bad, badly

bad—(adj) correctly used after a linking verb to describe the subject

I feel *bad* (sad) about what happened.

The child was *bad* (unruly) all day.

badly—(adv) Use after an action verb

She reacted *badly* to the announcement.

Do not use *badly* to mean *urgently, very much, greatly,* or *extremely* or to modify verbs denoting *want* or *need*.

The office *urgently* (not *badly*) needs reorganization.

She wants *very much* (not *badly*) to take a December vacation.

balance

(n) the amount remaining on the credit or debit side of an account

Do not use to mean *rest* or *remainder* in a nonfinancial sense.

He has a large *balance* in his checking account.

The *rest* (not the *balance*) of the books need to be cataloged.

because of, due to
Do not use interchangeably.
because of—(prep) used to introduce a prepositional phrase indicating reason
> *Because of* the weather he canceled his trip.

due to—(adj) caused by, resulting from. Used most frequently after a form of the verb *to be.*
> The accident was *due to* his careless driving.

being as, being that
Do not use either of these colloquial expressions as substitutes for *because.*
> COLLOQUIAL: *Being that* he will be in Chicago...
> CORRECT: *Because* he will be in Chicago...

beside, besides
beside—(prep) at the side of, next to
> She sat *beside* me at the concert.

besides—(prep) in addition to
> *Besides* completing the budget, we must consider four other projects.

be sure and, be sure to
Be sure and is considered both colloquial and unidiomatic. Use *be sure to...*
> *Be sure to* sign and return the enclosed contract.

The same is true of *come* and *try.*
> *Come to* (not *come and*) meet the president.
> *Try to* (not *try and*) finish the report on time.

between   See among, between.

biannual, biennial, semiannual, bimonthly, semimonthly
biannual—(adj) occurring twice a year
biennial—(adj) occurring every two years
semiannual—(adj) occurring twice a year at six-month intervals
bimonthly—(adj) occurring every two months
semimonthly—(adj) occurring twice a month

both
(pron) two
Often used unnecessarily.
> The two computers are alike (not *both* alike) in capacity.
> Are these computers (not *both* these computers) similar in performance?
> They will work together (not *both* work together) on the project.

bring, take
bring—(v) Use when the action is directed toward the speaker.
> *Bring* it here when you come.

take—(v) Use when the action is directed away from the speaker.
> *Take* these papers to Chicago when you go.

but...however
Use one or the other but not both.

INCORRECT:	The atmosphere was depressing, *but* the food was good, *however*.
CORRECT:	The atmosphere was depressing, *but* the food was good.
CORRECT:	The atmosphere was depressing; *however*, the food was good.

can, could, may, might

can—(v) expresses ability to act
> *Can* you meet that deadline?

expresses ability to be acted on
> The papers *can* be sent to the office.

could—(v) expresses possibility
> The caller *could* be he.

expresses conditional ability
> If you agree, he *could* install the equipment today.

expresses past ability
> When Mr. Smith was younger, he *could* speak Italian.

may—(v) expresses permission
> *May* I use your name as a reference?

expresses possibility
> We *may* be able to increase our use of noncommercial timber.

might—(v) expresses possibility with doubt
> You *might* be able to reach him at the office.

The substitution of *can* for *may* is colloquial English.
> COLLOQUIAL: *Can* I tell him to request an advance.
> WRITTEN BUSINESS ENGLISH: *May* I tell him you are in?

cannot

Always written as one word.
> She *cannot* attend tomorrow's luncheon.

can't hardly, can't scarcely See double negatives.

can't (cannot) help but

After *can't* use either *help* or *but* but not both.
> INCORRECT: I *can't help but* wonder why he called.
> CORRECT: I *can't help* wondering why he called.
> CORRECT: I *cannot but* wonder why he called.

capital, capitol, Capitol

capital—(adj) involving or calling for the death penalty
> Some states are moving toward *capital* punishment for certain crimes.

relating to wealth
> He made a *capital* investment of $85,000.

uppercase
> Every sentence begins with a *capital* letter.

capital—(n) the seat of government or the hub of an industry
> New York City is the financial *capital* of the United States.
> Trenton is the *capital* of New Jersey.

wealth or property
> His *capital* is invested in real estate.

capitol—(n) the building in which a state legislature meets

Capitol—(n) The building in which Congress meets, located in Washington DC.

Glossary of Usage

cite, sight, site

cite—(v) refer to; state

> She *cited* The Constitution as her authority,

sight—(n) scene, vision

> After the operation, his *sight* was fully restored.

site—(n) location

> Have they chosen a new *site* for the terminal?

come, go

come—(v) move toward the speaker

> *Come* to my office at 6 PM.

go—(v) move away from the speaker

> *Go* to the treasurer's office for the meeting.

See also **be sure and, be sure to.**

compare, contrast

compare—(v) represent as similar

> Her suggestions *compare* favorably with yours, but cost less.

contrast—(v) set in opposition in order to show differences

> The white couch *contrasts* with the blue walls.

For the correct prepositions in idiomatic constructions, see page 96.

complement, compliment, compliments

complement—(v) make complete

> Your designs will *complement* our office layout.

(n) something that completes or brings to perfection

> That painting is just the right *complement* to the living room.

compliment—(v) praise

> I want to *compliment* you on the fine job you have done.

(n) something said in praise

> Thank you for the lovely *compliment.*

compliments—(n) regards; good wishes

> Please accept the enclosed material with our *compliments.*

consensus

(n) general agreement

> The *consensus* is that we have to expand the firm.

Avoid using *consensus of opinion*, which is redundant.

consul, council, counsel

consul—(n) government official residing abroad who represents his country's commercial interests

> The French *consul* hosted a reception for local officials.

council—(n) official body designated to serve in a legislative, administrative, or advisory capacity

> The City *Council* will vote on that tomorrow.

counsel—(v) advise

counsel—(n) legal adviser

> Find someone to *counsel* you about the incident; in fact, ask your lawyer to act as your *counsel.*

continually, continuously
continually—(adv) repeated regularly and frequently
> She is *continually* inventing excuses for her absences.

continuously—(adv) continuing without interruption
> He talked *continuously* for over an hour.

contrast See **compare, contrast.**

could have, could of
After *could, ought to, might, should, would, may,* and *must,* use the helping verb have. The use of the word *of* after these verbs is incorrect. Also incorrect is *could've*, which sounds like *could of* and is also incorrect.

> INCORRECT: They *could of* finished by now.
> CORRECT: They *could have* finished by now.
> CORRECT: They *might have* gone to the conference room.

credible, creditable
credible—(adj) believable.
> The testimony presented by the prosecution was quite *credible.*

creditable—(adj) praiseworthy
> His performance under duress was *creditable.*

data
(n) The word *data* is plural and is treated as plural in scientific writing. In business writing it is usually treated as singular. The singular *datum* is seldom used.
> The *data* have been carefully collected. (in science)
> This *data* has been thoroughly checked. (in business)

descend, descent, dissent
descend—(v) come down
> He *descended* to the parking garage in his private elevator.

descent—(n) a decline
> The road made a sharp and dangerous *descent.*

dissent—(n) disagreement
> His was the only vote of *dissent* on the committee.

dissent—(v) to disagree
> Only one person *dissented.*

different, differently
different—(adj) not alike
> His voice sounds *different* tonight.

differently—(adv) in a different manner
> I wish we had done it *differently.*

different from, different than See page 96.

disburse, disperse
disburse—(v) pay out
> The treasurer will *disburse* any extra money.

disperse—(v) scatter; distribute widely
> The crowd quickly *dispersed* after the show.

Glossary of Usage

disinterested, uninterested

disinterested—(adj) impartial; unbiased

> We need to assign a *disinterested* person to this investigation.

uninterested—(adj) indifferent

> She seemed *uninterested* in the outcome of the trial.

done, don't

done—(v) past participle of *do*; must be used with helping verbs *has, have,* or *had.*

> CORRECT: I *have done* all the filing. They *have done* the work.
> INCORRECT: We *done* our work carefully.
> CORRECT: We *did* our work carefully.

contraction of *do not* Often used incorrectly for *doesn't.*

> It *doesn't* matter to me. (SINGULAR)
> They *don't* work hard enough. (PLURAL)

Neither contraction is normally acceptable in business writing.

double negatives

Only one negative word should be used to express a single negative idea. With such negative words as *barely, hardly, scarcely,* and *but* (meaning *only*), the use of *not* is incorrect.

> CORRECT: We *can hardly* refuse his request.
> INCORRECT: We *can't hardly* refuse his request.

> CORRECT: We *have but* one choice in this matter.
> INCORRECT: We *haven't but* one choice in this matter.

due to See **because of, due to.**

each other, one another

each other—(pron) refers to two persons or things

> Harris and John will help *each other* with their budgets.

one another—(pron) refers to two or, more often, more than two

> If we all help *one another,* we can finish early.

eager See **anxious, eager.**

effect See **affect, effect.**

elicit, illicit

elicit—(v) bring forth; provoke

> His proposal will *elicit* much controversy.

illicit—(adj) not permitted; illegal

> Traffic in *illicit* drugs is difficult to control.

emigrate, immigrate

emigrate—(v) go out of one country or region to settle in another

> When they *emigrated* from Russia, they left behind everything they owned.

immigrate—(v) come into a new country or region to settle there

> The country was settled by people who *immigrated* there to escape intellectual and religious persecution.

eminent, imminent

eminent—(adj) high; lofty; distinguished

   She is an *eminent* writer and lecturer.

imminent—(adj) likely to happen without delay

   A severe snowstorm is *imminent.*

ensure   See **assure, ensure, insure.**

envelop, envelope

envelop—(v) cover; wrap

   Fire will soon *envelop* the entire building.

envelope—(n) a covering; a wrapper

   Be sure to put all the enclosures inside the same *envelope.*

equally as

Do not use together.

INCORRECT:	She plays *equally as* well.
CORRECT:	She plays *as* well as he.
CORRECT:	They play *equally* well.

etc.

Abbreviation of et cetera, in Latin meaning *and so forth.*

May be used in informal writing when the reader can easily fill in what is omitted.

In more formal writing use expressions such as *and so forth, and so on,* or *and the like.*

INFORMAL:	The firm manufactures nuts, bolt, screws, nails, *etc.* at its main plant.
FORMAL:	The firm manufactures nuts, bolts, screws, nails, *and the like.*

Etc. and any of its equivalents are redundant when a list has been introduced by the expressions *such as* or *for instance,* which serve the same purpose of indicating that the list is not complete.

   The firm manufactures many small metal building materials, *such as* nuts, bolts, screws, and nails.

everyday, every day

everyday—(adj) ordinary; daily

   Always used before a noun: an *everyday* occurrence; one's *everyday* clothes.

every day—(adj + n)

   In all other contexts use two words. I eat an apple *every day.*

everyone, every one   See **anyone, any one.**

except   See **accept, except.**

farther, further

farther, farthest—(adj or adv) measurable distance

   His office is the *farthest* from the hospital.

   This car seems to go *farther* on premium gasoline.

further, furthest—(adj or adv) figurative distance in degree, quality, or time

   That report requires *further* study.

   Public recognition is the *furthest* thing from his mind.

fewer, less, lesser

fewer—(adj) answers the question How many? and modifies a plural noun
> *Fewer* persons attended the meeting than we had expected.

less—(adj) answers the question How much? and modifies a singular noun
> We spent *less* money on the project than we thought we would.

lesser—(adj) used in reference to value or importance
> The *lesser* sum is the correct one.

first

(adv) Use *first* to introduce a run-on enumeration; use *second* and *third*, not *secondly* and *thirdly*, to introduce subsequent items.
> *First*, outline the problem; *second*, list the possible solutions.

foreword, forward

foreword—(n) a preface or introductory note
> He finally completed the *foreword* to his book.

forward—(adv) movement onward
> The crowd surged *forward* to the stage.

formally, formerly

formally— in a formal manner
> We were asked to dress *formally* for the wedding.

formerly— at an earlier time
> She was *formerly* the director of personnel.

former, latter

Former and *latter*, respectively, refer to the first and the second of two persons or things mentioned.
> Carol Smith and John Nash have decided to join the firm. The *former* will arrive on May 1; the *latter*, on May 10.

If you are talking about more than two things, use *last*, not *latter*.
> She was the *last* to arrive.

formerly See **formally, formerly**.

further See **farther, further**.

go See **come, go**.

good, well

good—(adj) correctly used after a linking verb. *Good* is never used to modify a verb.
> I feel *good* about our investment. The play was quite *good*.

well—(adv) satisfactory or skillfully
> She types very *well* for a beginner.

well—(adj) in good health or suitable
> I don't feel *well* today.
> It was just as *well* I didn't go to the meeting.

To feel well is to be in good health. *To feel good* is to be in good spirits.

got, have got to
got—(v) colloquial when used to mean *must, ought, should*
  I *ought* (not *got*) to go.
have got to —a redundant and colloquial expression for *must*
  I must (not *have got to*) finish the project today.

hardly See **double negatives.**

healthful, healthy
healthful—(adj) beneficial to one's health
  Her diet is a *healthful* one.
healthy—(adv) enjoying good health
  I have been feeling *healthy* since I began to exercise.

hopefully
(adv) in a hopeful manner
  She waited *hopefully* for the letter to arrive.
In the sense of "it is to be hoped," the use of *hopefully* is debatable.
  Hopefully, we can come to an agreement.   (not universally accepted)

if, whether
if—(conj) used to introduce an adverbial clause of condition
  He will attend the meeting *if* it is held in Miami.
whether—(conj) used to introduce a noun clause
  Mr. Beck will tell us today *whether* he can attend the meeting.
In colloquial usage *if* and *whether* are used interchangeably.

illicit See **elicit, illicit.**

illusion See **allusion, illusion.**

immigrate See **emigrate, immigrate.**

imminent See **eminent, immanent, imminent.**

imply, infer
imply—(v) suggest something without specifically stating it
  He *implied* that he thought the plan would be too expensive.
infer—(v) come to a conclusion; interpret; judge from evidence
  From what he said we *infer* that an announcement is imminent.
A speaker or writer *implies*; a listener, reader, or observer *infers*.

inform See **advice, advise, inform.**

ingenious, ingenuous
ingenious—talented; resourceful; clever
  He developed an *ingenious* method for food processing.
ingenuous—innocent; naive
  She showed in her remarks that she was quite *ingenuous*.

in, in to, into

in—(prep) inside; within

> Mr. Bates is *in* his office.

> She is traveling *in* Italy.

in to—(adv + infinitive) He stopped *in to tell* us about his promotion. (*in* order *to tell*)

into—(prep) to the inside of; to the condition or form of.

> Mr. Smith has gone *into* Mr. Ellis's office.

> The proposal will be divided *into* three parts.

in regards to

incorrect. Use *in regard to, with regard to,* or *as regards.*

inform See **advice, advise, inform.**

insure See **assure, ensure, insure.**

into See **in, in to, into.**

irregardless

nonstandard. The correct word is *regardless.*

irritate See **aggravate, irritate.**

it, there

it —As a subject, this pronoun is correctly used in reference to time and weather.

> *It* is almost nine o'clock.

> *It* is raining outside.

it, there—Either of these can be used as an expletive, a word that occupies the position of the subject but has no meaning of its own. Because this construction delays the meaningful part of the sentence, use expletives sparingly in business writing.

DELAYED SUBJECT:	*It* is a pleasure to serve on this committee.
BETTER:	To serve on this committee is a pleasure.
DELAYED SUBJECT:	*There* are nine members on the committee.
BETTER:	Nine members make up the committee.
BETTER:	The committee comprises nine members.

its, it's

its—(possessive) <u>Never</u> has an apostrophe

> The cat is licking *its* bowl clean.

it's—(contraction) means it is or it has

> *It's* time to go home.

Use contractions sparingly, if at all, in business writing.

kind of, sort of, type of

Kind , sort, and *type* are singular nouns and are correctly modified by *this* or *that.*

> That *kind of* policy is favored by young executives.

Kinds, sorts, and *types* are plural nouns and are correctly modified by *these* or *those.*

> We no longer manufacture *those types of* fittings.

Do not use *kind of* or *sort of* to replace such adverbs as *somewhat* or *rather.*

> We are *somewhat* late in replying to his proposal. (not *sort of*)

Do not use the articles *a* or *an* after *kind of* and *sort of.*

> That *kind of* paint is no longer legal in this state. (not *kind of a*)

late, last, latest
late—(adj or adv) not on time; dead
> He was two hours *late* for the meeting.
> The late Senator Smith was honored at the ceremony.

last—superlative form of late; refers to the final item in a series
> She was *last* in line.

latest—another superlative form of *late;* means *the most recent*
> The Uprising is his *latest* novel; we hope it's not his *last.*

latter   See **former, latter.**

lay, lie
lay—(v) put or place. Principal parts—*lay, laid, laid, laying.* In the active voice, *lay* always has an object.
> Mr. Baldwin *lays* great *stress* on punctuality. (*stress* IS THE OBJECT)
> They are *laying* the *foundation* today. (*foundation* IS THE OBJECT)
> The cornerstone was *laid* in 1994.
> The stone will be *laid* by April 1.

lie—(v) rest or recline. Principal parts—*lie, lay, lain, lying.*
> The mail is *lying* on your desk.
> The book had *lain* unnoticed on the top of the file.
> The responsibility will *lie* with Mr. Burns's office.
> Yesterday the catalog *lay* on Ms. Ryan's desk.

lead, led
lead—(n) a metal
> *Lead* will protect you from X-rays.

led—(v) past tense and past participle of the verb *lead*
> He has *led* our company in our drive to increase market share.

leave, let
leave—(v) depart; abandon.
> I *leave* at eight every morning.
> I will *leave* the papers with you.

let—(v) allow. Will you *let* me help you complete the project?

lend, loan
Lend is a verb; *loan* is a noun that is sometimes used as a verb, particularly by financial institutions.
> If you will *lend* me the money, I will repay the *loan* by June.
> The bank became reluctant to *loan* money when the economy turned down.

less, lesser   See **fewer, less, lesser.**

liable to   See **apt to, liable to, likely to.**

like   See **as, like.**

likely to   See **apt to, liable to, likely to.**

Glossary of Usage

lose, loose
lose—(v) be unable to find
> If you are careful, you will not *lose* your way.

loose—(adj) not fastened down; not tight
> The floor board is *loose*.

ly adverbs
Separate two or more *ly adverbs*.
> AWKWARD: We are *usually particularly* rushed in December.
> BETTER: *Usually,* we are *particularly* rushed in December.
> BETTER: In December we *usually* are *particularly* rushed.

makeup, make up
makeup—(n or adj) cosmetics; nature; disposition
> She put on *makeup* for the play.
> The *makeup* exam is scheduled for November 15.

make up—(v + adv) compensate
> I will *make up* the work I missed.

may, might See **can, could, may, might**.

maybe, may be
maybe—(adv) perhaps
> *Maybe* the takeover will be announced today.

may be—(v) shows possibility
> It *may be* that we will scale back the program.

meantime
Use **meanwhile** or **in the meantime**.
> CORRECT: *In the meantime* I will collate the report.
> COLLOQUIAL: *Meanwhile* I will collate the report.

media
Very careful writers will use this noun only as a plural, although its use in the singular is widely accepted.
> Other *media are* being considered for the ad campaign.
> The *media is* relentless in pursuit of this story.

might of See **could of**.

more important, more importantly
more important—(introductory or transitional expression)
> *More important,* the deadline is now June 1.

more importantly—(adv)
> Mr. Jones was treated *more importantly* than I was.

most See **almost, most**.

nobody, no body
nobody—(pron) no person
> *Nobody* was at the receptionist's desk when I arrived.

no body—(adj + pron) no group
> *No body* of soldiers fought more bravely than our first battalion.

number   See **amount, number.**

off
Do not use *off of* or *off from* in place of *off*
> The passenger got *off* the train two stops too soon. (not *off of*)

one another   See **each other, one another.**

on, onto, on to   See **in, into, in to.**

paid, payed
paid—(v) past tense and past participle of *pay*
> He *paid* promptly.

payed—(v) past tense and past participle of *pay,* used to mean let out a rope or cable gradually and, in a very limited sense, to mean "coat with pitch to make waterproof."

passed, past
passed—(v) past tense and past participle of pass
> He *passed* the car to the right.

past— (n) time before the present
> In the *past* we needed fewer employees.

past —(adj) no longer current
> In *past* times we were treated like valued clients.

per, a
per—(prep) for each or for every
Substitute *a* or *an* whenever possible.
> The New York State speed limit is 65 miles *an* (not *per*) hour.

(prep) in accordance with. An English version is always preferred over the Latin *per.*
> Here are the documents *that you requested.* (not *per your request*)

personal, personnel
personal—(adj) private, individual
> I requested a *personal* interview with him.

personnel—(n) a body of employees
> All company *personnel* were notified of the changes. (treated as plural)

precede, proceed
precede—(v) go before
> Mr. Smith spoke more eloquently than those who *preceded* him.

proceed—(v) advance; go on.
> *Proceed* down the hall until you reach the stairs.

principal, principle
principal—(n) chief or head, specifically of a school or business organization
> Mr. Gilroy is the *principal* of the middle school.

principal—(n) a financial term meaning an amount of debt or investment minus outstanding interest
> He decided to live on the interest without touching his *principal.*

principal—(adj) first in rank, authority, or importance
>She will be the *principal* speaker.

principle—(n) a fundamental truth; a rule; moral standard
>She would not sacrifice her *principles* for financial gain.
>She stood on her *principles*.

prior to
Use *before*, which is less stilted than *prior to*. See me *before* (not *prior to*) the meeting.

proceed   See **precede, proceed.**

proved, proven
proved—(v) demonstrated convincingly
>He *proved* that the plan would save money.

proven—(adj) proved; verified
>We have a *proven* plan to save money.

provided, providing
provided—(conj) equivalent of *if*
>You can save money *provided* you follow our simple plan.

providing—(present participle) giving or offering
>Redwood enclosures, *providing* privacy and attractive fencing, are frequently
>seen in the suburbs.

quiet, quite
quiet—(adj) not noisy; silent
>Be *quiet* when the microphone is on.

quite—(adv) to a considerable degree
>She was *quite* concerned when the plane didn't arrive.

raise, rise
raise—(v) cause to rise; collect; rear or grow. Principal parts—*raise, raised, raising*.
Raise always has an object.
>We must *raise* $10,000 to cover the cost of the renovation.

rise—(v) move or extend upward. Principal parts—*rise, rose, rising, risen*.
>Prices often *rise* at this time of year.

real, really, sure, surely
Real and *sure* are adjectives. *Really* and *surely* are adverbs. If *certainly* or *very* can be
substituted, use *really* or *surely*.
>Your exhibit at the show was *really* impressive. (not *real*)
>You will *surely* be rewarded. (not *sure*)

reason is that
Use *that*, not *because*, to introduce a noun clause after the expression *the reason is*.
>The reason I hired her is *that* she has more experience. (not *because*)

recommend, refer
recommend—(v) suggest favorably
>He *recommended* our firm to handle the account.

refer—(v) direct attention to
>Please *refer* to page 16 in the annual report.

respectfully, respectively
respectfully—(adj) with deference
> They treat their employees *respectfully*.

respectively—(adv) in the order named
> Ann and Tom were named president and vice president, *respectively*.

said (adj)
Except in legal usage do not use expressions such as *the said client* when you mean t*his client* or *the client mentioned above*. In most cases the reference is clear without any additional explanation.

same (pron)
Do not use *same* to refer to a previously mentioned thing.
> We have shipped your order, and you will receive it by Friday. (*it* not *same*)

scarcely   See **double negatives**.

semiannual, semimonthly   See **biannual, bimonthly**.

serve, service (verbs) You serve people but service things.
> We *serve* our customers conscientiously.
> We *service* our customers' equipment carefully.

set, sit
set—(v)   put or place something in position; establish. (Must have a direct object.)
> She *set up* a new filing system.
> Please *set* the table for two.

sit—(v)   rest; assume a sitting position. A person sits voluntarily; a thing sits where it has been placed. (Does not have a direct object.)
> The caller *sat* in the reception room for hours.
> The package *has sat* there all afternoon.

shall, should, will, would
Except in very formal speech and writing *will* and *would* are used to express the future and conditional in all three persons.
> VERY FORMAL: I *shall* (or *should*) be glad to review the final copy.
> LESS FORMAL: I *will* (or *would*) be glad to review the final copy.

shall—(v)   in all three persons signifies control by some authority
> The bylaws state that he as chairman *shall* preside.
> She is determined that her daughter *shall* assume more managerial responsibility.

would, should—(v)   imply conditional circumstance or uncertainty. *Would* expresses past action as well. *Should* can also express moral obligation.
Uncertainty: I *would* provide an office for you if you *should* decide to take the job.
Past action: Mr. Johnson *would* always fly when he went to Washington.
Obligation: Everyone *should* comply with the terms of the agreement.

will, would—(v)   denote willingness, promise, and intention.
> We *will* gladly accommodate your party at eight o'clock.
> We *would* be honored to accommodate you.

Glossary of Usage

sight, site   See **cite.**

so, so that
so—(conj) therefore.
Somewhat informal. Better to use *therefore*.
>   INFORMAL: The work is finished, *so* you can dismiss the crew.
>   BETTER: The work is finished; *therefore*, the crew can go home.
so that—(conj) in order that
>   He arrived early *so that* (or *so*)he could finish the work.

someday, some day
someday—(adv) Use when you can eliminate *someday* from the sentence without
altering its meaning.
>   Set up a meeting *someday* next week.
some day—(adj + n) Use as the object of a preposition.
>   Set the meeting for *some day* next week.

someone, some one   See **anyone.**

some time
some time—(adj + n) an indefinite amount of time
>   He spent *some time* working on the project.
>   *For some time* we have been considering the job.
>   *Some time* ago we quoted them a price on supplies.

sometime, sometimes
sometime—(adv) at an unspecified time
Use *sometime* as one word when you can eliminate it from the sentence.
>   Please come to see the demonstration *sometime*.
sometimes—(adv) occasionally
>   *Sometimes* she substitutes for my secretary.

sort of   See **kind of.**

stationary, stationery
stationary—(adj) fixed in position; unchanging
>   The interest rate has remained *stationary* for the last six months.
stationery—(n) writing materials, especially paper and envelopes
>   Office *stationery* should be plain but of good quality.

sure, surely   See **real, really, sure, surely.**

take   See **bring, take.**

than, then
than—(conj) used to introduce the second element in a comparison
>   Our profits were higher *than* we had expected them to be.
then—(adv) at that time; next in order
>   We will prepare our proposal and *then* make an appointment to see you.

that, which   See **relative pronouns**, pages 84–85.

their, there, they're
their—(possessive adj) belonging to
>They gave us *their data* last night.

there—(adv) at or in that place
>I will try to be *there* by eight o'clock.

There is also an expletive and as such is best avoided in written business English.
See more under *it. there.*
they're—(contraction) they are.
>*They're* sending us the revised figures. (INFORMAL)

theirs, there's
theirs—(possessive pron) <u>Never</u> has an apostrophe.
>The car is *theirs.*

there's—(contraction)
>*There's* a fly in my soup.

try and   See **be sure and, be sure to.**

type of   See **kind of.**

uninterested   See **disinterested, uninterested.**

up
This adverb is often used unnecessarily after verbs such as *rest, end, join, hurry,* and *settle.*
In business writing omit *up* when it does not add to the meaning of the sentence.
>*Divide* the work between the two clerks. (not *divide up*)
>He plans to rest next Monday. (not *rest up*)

way, ways
way—(n) path, route, or direction
>You must make *way* for a fire truck.

ways—(n) Colloquial substitute for *way.* Do not use in business writing.
>INCORRECT: I have a long *ways* to go.
>CORRECT: I have a long *way* to go.

weather, whether
weather—(n) climate
>The *weather* should be favorable.

whether—(conj) if it be the case; introduces a noun clause
>I wonder *whether* Andrew Jones will declare his candidacy.

well   See **good, well.**

whereas   See **although, whereas, while.**

whether   See **if, whether;** also **weather, whether.**

which   See **that, which.**

while   See **although, whereas, while.**

who, whom   See **relative pronouns,** pages 84-85.

who's, whose
who's—(contraction) A short form of *who is* or *who has.*
> *Who's* in charge of this department? (INFORMAL)

whose—(possessive adj)
> *Whose* are these?
> She is the applicant *whose* résumé I discussed with you yesterday.

will, would   See **shall, should, will, would.**

you're, your
you're—(contraction) a short form for *you are.*
> Please call me by Friday to let me know whether *you're* willing to accept the position. (INFORMAL)

your—(possessive adj)
> I would appreciate *your* assessment of the situation.

CHAPTER 8 Parts of a Business Letter

CHAPTER 8 **Parts of a Business Letter**

A business letter has four principal parts: the heading, the opening, the body, and the closing. This chapter explains the elements of information that these parts may contain and where to position them.

The body of the letter will, of course, follow the punctuation rules explained in Chapter 5. For the heading, opening, and closing you may use either **mixed** (or standard) **punctuation,** in which the salutation is followed by a colon and the complimentary close is followed by a comma, or **open punctuation,** which eliminates all punctuation except for the body of the letter.

Either style of punctuation is acceptable with any letter format.

Contents

The Parts of a Letter and Their Relative Positions

Letter Styles

Parts of a Business Letter

Interoffice Memorandums

Envelopes

LETTERHEAD
_____

Date

SPECIAL NOTATION

Name and Title
Firm Name
Street Address
City, State Zip Code

Attention Line

Salutation:

Subject Line or File Reference

Body of Letter

_____
_____
_____
_____
_____ .

_____
_____
_____
_____

Complimentary closing,

COMPANY NAME

Typed Signature, Title

Reference Initials

Enclosure

Mailing Instructions
Copy Notation

P.S.

Dictator's Initials

The Body of the Letter

The body of the letter usually begins a double space below the salutation or the subject line. If the body of the letter is double-spaced, indent the first word of each paragraph.

In an average letter paragraphs from four to six lines are preferable. No paragraph should be over eight lines. A very short paragraph is sometimes used for emphasis but loses its emphatic value if used more than once in the same letter.

Letter Placement Tab

Letter Length	Words in Body	Side Margins	Lines Below Date Line
Short	Up to 100	2 inches	8-10
Medium	100-150	1 1/2 inches	8
	150-175		6
	175-200		4
Long	Over 200 (or more than one page	1 inch	4-6

The approximate number of words in a letter can be gauged by multiplying the number of lines of shorthand or speedwriting notes by the average number of words on a line.

Spacing and Indentation

Material to be Typed	Spacing	Indentation
All but very short letters	Single	Block or 5 spaces
Very short letters	Double	5 spaces
Legal Papers	Double	10 spaces
Reports, manuscripts, specifications, editorials	Double or triple	5 spaces

Full Block Style
Letterhead
Date
Mailing Information
Special Notations

Katharine Gibbs School
717 Fifth Avenue
New York, NY 11017

January 27, 19—

CONFIDENTIAL

Mr. Daniel Jayson Stern
Executive Vice-President
Stern, Stern, and Wilson
1097 Centre Street
Chicago, IL 09876

Dear Mr. Stern:

Letterhead. The printed letterhead of a company consists of the firm name and the mailing address. It may also include the telephone number, the names of executives, and a company symbol or trademark. When printed letterhead is not used, type in single space the complete mailing address. Start at the top of the frame of your computer screen to leave a 1-inch margin. Center each line on the page.

Date. The date of the letter should be the date on which the letter was dictated, not transcribed. Although the 15th line is often called the dateline, the placement may vary from 12 to 18 lines from the top, depending on the length of the letter.

Mailing Information. When you send a letter by a method other than regular mail, type such information in full caps a double space below the date line. Type any additional mailing information on the next line. If the letter also contains a special notation, type the mailing notation a double space below the reference initials or enclosure notation.

Special Notations. Type a special notation, such as PERSONAL or CONFIDENTIAL, in full caps at the left margin two or three lines below the date line.

Very truly yours,

Diane K. Lang
Human Resources Director

DKL:re

REGISTERED MAIL

Part of a Business Letter

Modified Block Style
Inside Address
Subject Line

Katharine Gibbs School
717 Fifth Avenue
New York, NY 11017
212-777-0987

January 27, 19—

Mrs. Toni Brown, Vice-President
Brown Associates, Incorporated
17 Marlowe Avenue, Suite 405
Tallahassee, FL 09008-0763

Dear Mrs. Brown:

Subject: Parts of a Business Letter

Inside Address. The inside address is single-spaced and blocked at the left margin. It begins from four to eight lines below the dateline, depending on the length of the letter. The inside address consists of the name of the person or company and the mailing address. Do not underscore names of newspapers or magazines. Place the apartment, floor, or suite number after the street address. Type the city, state, and ZIP Code on the last line, leaving two spaces between the state and ZIP Code.

Whenever possible, address a letter to a specific person. Type the person's name on the first line of the inside address (or just a title if the name is not known). The business or executive title can be placed after the name of the person on the first line, alone on the second line, or before the company or department name—whichever will best achieve uniformity of line length.

Subject Line. Use a subject line to summarize the contents of a letter for the convenience of the reader or to refer to related correspondence. It may be centered or blocked a double space below the salutation. If indented paragraphs are used, it may also be indented.

The terms *Subject:, In re:, or Re:* may precede the subject but are not necessary. The last two are generally not used except in legal correspondence. Type the subject line either in full capitals or initially capped and underscored.

Sincerely yours,

Marion Hendrickson
Marketing Manager

Modified Block Style
with Indented Paragraphs
Attention Line
Salutation

Katharine Gibbs School
717 Fifth Avenue
New York, NY 11017
212-777-0987

January 27, 19—

Englewood Lumber Company
11 East Englewood Avenue
Englewood, NJ 07631

Attention: Mr. David O. Rice

Dear Sir or Madam:

    Attention line. An attention line is used to direct a letter (addressed to a company) to a particular department, to a person with whom the writer has had previous correspondence, or to someone qualified to deal with the subject matter of the letter.

    Since the letter is addressed to a company, using the attention line ensures that the letter will be opened and the contents handled if the person to whom the letter is directed is not available. The correct salutation in a letter with an attention line is *Dear Sir* or *Madam:* Type the attention line flush with the left margin, a double space below the last line of the address and a double space above the salutation. Type it in initial caps with underscore or in full caps without underscore—for example,

ATTENTION: PURCHASING AGENT.

    Salutation. Type the salutation flush with the left margin a double space below the inside address or attention line. Capitalize the first word, the name, and the title in the salutation. Follow it with a colon unless you are using open punctuation. The salutation must agree with the first line of the address, not with the attention line.

Sincerely,

Janet P. Kenny
Manager

JPK:mk

Modified Block Style with Block Paragraphs

Complimentary Closing
Reference Initials
Enclosure Notation
Copy Notation
Two-Page Letter Headings
Postscript

Katharine Gibbs School
717 Fifth Avenue
New York, NY 11017
212-777-0987

January 27, 19—

Mrs. Wilhelmina Wilkins
Manager, Taft Hotel
1234 Jason Avenue
Great Neck, NY 11050

Dear Mrs. Wilkins:

SUBJECT: MORE PARTS OF THE BUSINESS LETTER

Complimentary closing. The complimentary closing is typed two spaces below the last line of the body of the letter. When you write as a representative of a firm, type the company name in full capitals a double space below the complimentary closing. Allow four lines for the handwritten signature between the company name and the typed signature of the writer.

When the letterhead is considered sufficient identification or when the letter is being sent from the executive office, the company signature is often omitted.

Reference initials (the initials of the writer and the typist) are typed at the left margin two spaces below the last line of the typed signature. They identify the person who dictated the letter and the person who transcribed it. The writer's initials are typed first; the transcriber's, second. Initials are omitted when the writer types his/her own letter. All of the following are acceptable:

LRB:AK   LRB/AK   LRB:ak   LRB/ak

Enclosure Notation. When an item or items are to be sent with a letter, type an enclosure notation at the left margin a double space below the identifying initials. If more than one item is enclosed, you may specify the number. You may also choose to specify the items enclosed. The following are all acceptable:

Enclosure	Enclosures	Enclosures 2
	Enc. 2	

Enclosures: 1. Check for $80 2. December Statement	Enclosures: Check for $80 December Statement

Copy notation. A copy notation indicates that a copy of the letter is being sent to someone other than the addressee. Type it a double space below the reference initials or the enclosure notation. If you do not wish to show that a copy is being sent to someone else, place a blind copy (bc) notation in the upper left corner of the copy.

bc S. R. Brown

Two-page letters. In a two-page letter, page 1 should end with a 1-inch bottom margin. Try to divide between paragraphs. If not possible, the last paragraph of the first page and the first paragraph of the second page should each contain at least two lines of typing. Do not hyphenate the last word on the first page. Type page 2 on plain paper of the same quality, color, and size as the letterhead paper. Top and side margins should be 1 inch. The heading on page 2 and on succeeding pages should consist of the first line of the inside address, the page number, and the date. It may be typed vertically (as shown above) or horizontally:

Mrs. Wilhelmina Wilkins   Page 2   January 27, 19—

When a letter addressed to a company has an attention line, the name of the heading is that of the company, not the name on the attention line. Double-space after the heading before continuing the body of the letter.

Sincerely,

KATHARINE GIBBS SCHOOL

Maryanne Davies, Director

MD:KL
Enclosure

c J. L. Morse

P.S.   A **postscript** is used to give a point special emphasis or to include an important afterthought or information not available before the transcription of the letter. It may be preceded by P.S., PS, or PS: ; or the abbreviation may be omitted. Type it two to four lines (as space permits) below the last line of typing. Indent or block it to agree with the style of the body of the letter. Either on the same line or two spaces below, type the dictator's initials.

M.D.

Simplified Style

Katharine Gibbs School
717 Fifth Avenue
New York, NY 11017
212-777-0987

January 27, 19—

Ms. Jeannine Pugliese
One Knolls Lane
Matawan, NJ 44567

SIMPLIFIED LETTER STYLE

The simplified letter style was introduced by the Administrative Management Society (AMS).

In an AMS letter every line begins at the left margin. A subject line is typed in full capitals, a double space below the inside address; the word "Subject" is omitted. The body of the letter is typed a triple space below the subject line.

No salutation or complimentary closing is used. The signature is typed in full capitals on the fourth or fifth line below the last line of the message. The typist's initials are typed a double space below the writer's name.

JAMES W. WIDMARK
ASSISTANT MANAGER

RM

Executive Style

Katharine Gibbs School
717 Fifth Avenue
New York, NY 11017
212-777-0987

January 27, 19—

Dear Mr. Monroe:

The Executive style is appropriate for personal and semi-social business letters, such as letters of appreciation, congratulations, condolence, informal business invitations, and responses to typewritten business invitations. Executive-size (Monarch) stationery, 7 1/4 by 10 1/2 inches, is usually chosen for this type of letter.

The inside address is typed below the signature block and flush with the left margin. The executive style, like the modified block style, allows a choice between block and indented paragraphs.

Very truly yours,

Vice-President

Mr. James Monroe
Chairman
The Monroe Group
1717 Adams Avenue
Winchester, IL 29674

Enclosure

(Reference initials on copy only)

Typed and Written Signatures

Typing the writer's signature ensures legibility and identifies the writer on copies of the letter. Place the official title of the writer on the same line or on the next line after the typed signature of the writer.

Sincerely yours,

Ann R. Blake

Ann R. Blake
Dean of Secretarial Studies

Academic, military, and professional titles should appear in the typewriten signatures as illustrated:

Sincerely yours,   Very truly yours,

James F. Pelegano, M.S.   Robert E. McHugh
Assistant Professor   Sergeant, USAF

Yours truly,   Yours very truly,

Reverend Richard McHugh   Honorable Ellen G. Cole

If the gender of the name is not immediately apparent, include the appropriate courtesy title in the typed signature.

Sincerely yours,   Sincerely yours,

Mr. Madison Ryan   Miss Madison Green

If a woman does not use a special title, such as M.D. or Dean of Students, she may include her courtesy title in the typed signature. If she does not wish to indicate her marital status, she may omit the courtesy title altogether or use Ms.

Sincerely yours,   Sincerely yours,

Ann S. Riley   *Ann S. Riley*

Ms. Ann L. Riley   Ann L. Riley

A married woman using her maiden name for professional purposes may use either Miss or Ms.

A woman who wishes to use Mrs. may choose any one of the four styles given below for a woman whose maiden name is Clare A. Conti and whose husband's name is Roger D. Durkin.

Sincerely yours,   Sincerely yours,

Clare A. Durkin   *Clare C. Durkin*

Mrs. Clare A. Durkin   Mrs. Clare C. Durkin

Sincerely yours,   Sincerely yours,

Clare A. Durkin   *Clare Conti-Durkin*

Mrs. Clare Conti Durkin   Mrs. Clare A. Conti-Durkin

Including a husband's given name in the typed signature is considered an acceptable option only in social correspondence, not in business correspondence. A divorced woman never uses her former husband's given name in the typed signature.

When a letter requires two signatures, use either of the following forms:

Sincerely yours,

Harriet Jenkins

Ms. Harriet Jenkins
District Manager

Frederick Marshall

Frederick Marshall
General Manager

Sincerely yours,

Harriet Jenkins

Ms. Harriet Jenkins
District Manager

Frederick Marshall

Frederick Marshall
General Manager

Secretary's signature.   When a secretary signs a letter that he or she has written for the employer, the following form is correct.   Courtesy titles may be used with either or both names.

Very truly yours,

Marjorie M. Nelson

Marjorie M. Nelson
Secretary to John White

Very truly yours,

Marjorie Nelson

Miss Marjorie Nelson
Secretary to Mr. White

When a secretary signs for the employer, the following forms are correct:

Yours very truly,

Lester J. Knowles
J. a. W.

Lester J. Knowles, Supervisor
Accounting Department

Yours very truly,

Leslie Ann Wilkes

For Lester J. Knowles

When a letter is written and signed by a secretary and the name of the person who authorized the letter also appears in the signature group, the following form is correct.

Yours very truly,

Allen Holbrooke

MURCHISON FARMS, INC.
Louise Crawford, Manager

By Allen Holbrooke
Secretary to Ms. Crawford

Parts of a Business Letter

When responding to the preceding letter, use this form in the inside address:

Ms. Louise Crawford, Manager
Murchison Farms, Inc.
Benson, MI 49431-7125

ATTENTION: MR. ALLEN HOLBROOKE

Dear Ms. Crawford:

Envelopes

An envelope should be of the same quality and color as the letterhead paper. The No. 10 envelope (4 1/8 by 9 1/2 inches) is almost universally used for ordinary business letters, but smaller or larger envelopes may be used as well.

The envelope address must repeat exactly the inside address, including any mailing and /or personal notations.

Samples Envelopes

The Katharine Gibbs School
717 Fifth Avenue
New York, NY 11017

REGISTERED MAIL

CONFIDENTIAL

Mrs. Wilhelmina Wilkins
Manager, Taft Hotel
1234 Jason Avenue
Great Neck, NY 11050

The Katharine Gibbs School
717 Fifth Avenue
New York, NY 11017

Englewood Lumber Company
Attention: Mr. David O. Rice
11 East Englewood Avenue
Englewood, NJ 07631

The United States Postal Service (USPS) uses optical character recognition equipment and suggests the following guidelines to ensure readability:

> Use rectangular envelopes that provide a good color contrast with the type. Black type on white paper is best. Envelopes must be no smaller than 3 1/2 by 5 inches and no larger than 6 1/8 by 11 1/2 inches. Type all information in full caps and eliminate all punctuation.

> Use only those abbreviations listed in the "Address Abbreviations" section of the National ZIP Code Directory. Single-space the address block. Space twice before the Zip Code.

> The destination address block must be more than 1 inch from both the left and right edges and at least 5/8 inch, but not more than 3 inches, from the bottom of the envelope.

> Type the return address in block style in the upper left corner. Start three spaces from the left edge on line 2, and use single spacing.

(Your software package should automatically position the information on the envelope correctly.)

Sample of a USPS-Style Envelope

```
THE KATHARINE GIBBS SCHOOL
717 FIFTH AVENUE
NEW YORK, NY  11017
                                    REGISTERED MAIL


CONFIDENTIAL

              MRS. TONI BROWN VICE-PRESIDENT
              BROWN ASSOCIATES INCORPORATED
              17 MARLOWE AVENUE   SUITE 40
              TALLAHASSEE FL  09008
```

Special Mailing Information. The following examples show the correct envelope placement of an address with an *in care of* notation and addresses that require apartment, post-office box, room, and rural-delivery numbers.

Traditional Style	USPS Style
Mrs. Ross Prescott	MRS ROSS PRESCOTT
c/o Mrs. James Phelps	C/O MRS JAMES PHELPS
189 Beacon Street	189 BEACON STREET
Boston, MA 02109	BOSTON MA 02109
Mr. James R. Newhall	MR JAMES R NEWHALL
202 East Main Street, Apt. 4G	202 EAST MAIN STREET APT 4G
Providence, RI 02904	PROVIDENCE RI 02904
Messrs. Tower and Wade	MESSRS TOWER AND WADE
Post Office Box 145	POST OFFICE BOX 145
Montclair, NJ 07042	MONTCLAIR NJ 07042
Miss Rosemary Markwick	MISS ROSEMARY MARKWICK
Tyler Arcade	TYLER ARCADE
990 East 181st Street, Room 17	990 EAST 181ST STREET ROOM 17
Bronx, NY 10460	BRONX NY 10460

Mr. Donald Sargent	MR DONALD SARGENT
RFD 1	RFD 1
Lakewood, OH 44107	LAKEWOOD OH 44107

A post office box number and a street address may both be included, but the address where the mail is to be delivered must appear on the line immediately above the bottom line.

Mail will	GRAND PRODUCTS INC
be delivered	100 MAJOR ST
here →	PO BOX 200
	PORTLAND OR 97214

Mail will	GRAND PRODUCTS INC
be delivered	PO BOX 200
here →	100 MAJOR ST
	PORTLAND OR 97214

Foreign Mail.   Type the name of a foreign country in full capital letters as the last line of the address. In the inside address the name of the country is typed with an initial capital.

Traditional Style	**USPS Style**
Mr. Edward J. Cousins	MR EDWARD J COUSINS
15 Roxbury Street	15 ROXBURY STREET
London, E.C. 1	LONDON EC 1
ENGLAND	ENGLAND
Dr. Alfredo Perales	DR ALFREDO PERALES
Obregon Sur 108	OBREGON SUR 108
Saltillo, Coahuila	SALTILLO COAHUILA
MEXICO	MEXICO

Folding and Inserting Letters in Envelopes

For the large business envelope (No. 10), 8 1/2 by 11 paper, and for the Monarch envelope, executive-size paper:

Fold the sheet up from the bottom slightly less than one-third of its length. With the edges even at the sides, crease the fold.

Fold the top downward not quite one-third of the sheet to within approximately one-half inch of the first crease. With the edges even at the sides, crease the second fold.

Place the second folded edge into the envelope so that the one-half-inch margin shows at the top just under the flap.

For a window envelope:

Fold the sheet up from the bottom one-third of the length of the sheet.

Fold the top third of the sheet backward from the first fold so that the address will be on the outside.

Insert the letter into the envelope so that the address shows through the window.

Memorandum

Katharine Gibbs School

To: _____ Date: _____

From: _____ Subject: _____

Here are some guidelines for setting up internal memorandums:

Headings may be typed horizontally, as shown above, or vertically as follows. Except for *To:*, which is always first, the order of the headings may vary.

    To: _____

    From: _____

    Date: _____

    Subject: _____

Also acceptable is lining up the colons instead of the words and/or using uneven spacing after the colons so the first words of all headings line up.

Courtesy titles are usually omitted from memo headings, but professional titles are included.

Use block style for the body, lining up the paragraphs with the heading items.

Type the body of the memo a triple space below the last line of the heading.

Single-space within paragraphs; double-space between paragraphs.

Type the reference initials at the left margin a double space below the body of the memo.

Block and double-space any additional notations such as enclosures, copies, and so on.

The software program you or your company uses may provide a template for memorandums, in which case you will simply fill in the information in the spaces provided.

Interoffice Envelopes

When addressing an envelope containing an interoffice memorandum, include the personal title, name, business title, and department name of the addressee. This ensures that the envelope will be delivered to the intended person or to another person designated to receive all interoffice memorandums.

Many organizations use special envelopes for memorandums. If your organization does not, use a plain envelope but type COMPANY MAIL in capital letters in the postage location.

If the memorandum is personal or confidential, type the appropriate notation in full capital letters above the name of the addressee.

Sample of an Interoffice Business Envelope

```
                                              COMPANY MAIL




                    PERSONAL
                    Mrs. Eve Rouke
                    Director, Education Dept.
                    The Katharine Gibbs School
```

If the memorandum is addressed to several people, list the names on the envelope, and check the first name. Each addressee is expected to cross out his or her name, write the date, check the next name on the list, and pass the memorandum on to that person.

```
        ✓  ~~Richard Eiger~~   3|10
           Nancy Hall
           Rosanna Hansen
           Mark Russell
```

CHAPTER 9 **Effective Business Writing**

CHAPTER 9 **Effective Business Writing**

The Principles of Good Business Writing

E-mail, voice-mail, faxes, personal computers, on-line services—technology has drastically changed the way we communicate, and yet writing well is a skill that never goes out of fashion. Although technology has made the mechanical aspects of writing business correspondence easier, only a person can compose a well-written letter, memo, or report, tailored to a specific situation and conveying just the right meaning.

From the shortest memo to the longest report, every written business communication should strive to be clear, correct, concise, courteous, and complete.

Clear

Business writing should be easy to read and effortlessly understood. <u>If a message has to be read more than once, it's not clear enough.</u>

To make your writing clear. . .

Choose the better known of two words, and use more one-syllable than two- or three-syllable words.

Instead of	Say	Instead of	Say
ostensibly	apparently	commensurate with	equal to
cognizant	aware	equitable	fair
initiate	begin or start	finalize	finish
discrepancy	difference	initial	first
expiration	end	procure	get
terminate	end	render	give
sufficient	enough	preclude	prevent
equivalent	equal	transmit	send
minimal	small	recapitulate	summarize
utilize	use	communicate	write *or* call

Use specific words instead of general words.

Instead of	Say
furniture	chairs, desks, tables
office equipment	desk, file, personal computer
employee	salesperson, clerk, secretary
merchandise	boots, shoes, belts
color	aqua, mauve, red, blue
contact	write, phone, fax
feel	think, believe, am confident
do	write, research, compose
at an early date	
by return mail	soon, today, tomorrow
in due time	or
at your convenience	state exactly when
in the near future	

Use modern English instead of so-called business jargon.

Instead of	Say
per (as in $4 per dozen)	a or an ($4 a dozen; 23 patients an hour)
concerning in reference to regarding relative to with respect to pertaining to	about
in compliance with your request pursuant to your request	as you requested
line	business, trade, profession
per (as in a letter signature)	by
under separate cover	separately, by fax, by messenger
are (not) in a position to	can or cannot
enclosed please find	enclosed is
attached hereto	I have enclosed
enclosed herewith	the enclosed pamphlet, etc.
acknowledge receipt of are in receipt of	have received
encounter difficulty	have trouble
the undersigned, the writer	I
same	it, they, them
communication	letter, telegram, memo, fax, phone, e-mail
proposition	plan, proposal
do not hesitate	please
said plan, said person	this or that plan or person
we regret to say	we are sorry
we deem it advisable	we suggest
subsequent to your arrival	after you arrive
prior to your departure	before you leave
pursuant to our agreement	as we agreed

Avoid stuffy, overblown language. Avoid in vogue words like *legitimize, factionalize, profitwise, effectuate, parameter, interface, dichotomy,* or *polarization* in favor of simple, natural, conversational words.

Make your most important points stand out. Remember, anything appearing at the beginning or end of a sentence, a paragraph, or a letter will receive special emphasis. In addition, you can draw attention to important points with

1. White space (tabulate, indent)
2. Unusual word order

Instead of	Say
Students who register late are at a disadvantage.	At a disadvantage are students who register late.
Only a short distance from the hotel are the Statue of Liberty, the South Street Seaport, and Ellis Island.	The Statue of Liberty, the South Street Seaport, and Ellis Island—these are just a short distance from the hotel.

3. A very short sentence among longer ones
4. A single-sentence paragraph between longer ones
5. Pauses (punctuation)

Instead of	Say
The tired and discouraged man went home early.	The man, tired and discouraged, went home early.
The factory is now deserted and abandoned.	The factory is deserted now, abandoned.

6. Typography (caps, italics, boldface, parentheses, underlining)
7. ? and !
8. Active voice rather than passive voice
9. Concrete, not abstract, words

Instead of	Say
One should prepare oneself for the future.	Prepare yourself for the future.
Occupational opportunities are available.	Jobs are available.

Use tables, graphs, charts, and the like when doing so makes the data easier to read and to comprehend. Put these items in the body of the writing as close as possible to your discussion of the data.

Correct

Business writing must contain accurate information and follow accepted standards of grammar, spelling, punctuation, sentence construction, and setup. A reader may not immediately spot or be able to name the grammatical error, but the error often results in awkward and confusing writing.

To make your writing correct. . .

Punctuate correctly. Avoid sentence fragments—groups of words that do not express complete thoughts.

Incorrect	Correct
Because I need a pleasant and efficient person.	I need a pleasant and efficient person.

Avoid run-on sentences—sentences that run into each other because of missing or incorrect punctuation.

Incorrect	Correct
Yesterday I interviewed Carla Benson, I was impressed by her attitude and skills.	Yesterday, during my interview with Carla Benson, I was impressed by her attitude and skills.

Use parallel sentence structure. A coordinate conjunction must join two or more grammatically identical constructions. The effective use of parallelism in sentences enables the reader to quickly grasp the relationship between facts and ideas.

Incorrect	Correct
The antiques on display are *neither* appealing *nor* of value. (ADJECTIVE + PREPOSITIONAL PHRASE)	The antiques on display are *neither* appealing *nor* valuable. (ADJECTIVE + ADJECTIVE)
She told me to request a cash advance *and* that I should call her when I receive it. (INFINITIVE PHRASE + NOUN CLAUSE)	She told me to request a cash advance and to call her when I receive it. (INFINITIVE PHRASE + INFINITIVE PHRASE)
You *can not only* use your telephone credit card when you are at home *but also* when you travel. (VERB + ADVERBIAL CLAUSE)	You can use your telephone credit card *not only* when you are home *but also* when you travel (ADVERBIAL CLAUSE + ADVERBIAL CLAUSE)

Not only must the grammatical structure be parallel, but the ideas must be logically connected.

Incorrect	Correct
He changed the tape in the VCR and changed his mind about retiring. (ILLOGICAL RELATIONSHIP)	He changed the tape in the VCR and lowered the volume on the TV. (LOGICAL RELATIONSHIP)

Even in different sentences, similar ideas are expressed more effectively in parallel form.

Instead of	Say
It was the best of times. Times were bad.	It was the best of times. It was the worst of times.

Parallelism is also important in tabulations and other lists. All elements in the list must be of the same grammatical construction.

Incorrect	Correct
The guide includes the following information: 1. passport requirements 2. city maps 3. getting around 4. where to eat	The guide includes the following information: 1. passport requirements 2. city maps 3. transportation schedules 4. a list of restaurants

Avoid misplaced and dangling constructions.

Incorrect	Correct
To complete the questionnaire, careful research will be necessary.	To complete the questionnaire, we need to research the issues carefully.
(The infinitive phrase dangles: The research is not completing the questionnaire.)	(The infinitive phrase precedes the word *we*, the logical doer of the action.)
Winston Churchill celebrated his birthday by eating a 30-pound birthday cake along with his grandchildren.	Winston Churchill, along with his grandchildren, celebrated his birthday by eating a 30-pound cake.

Use pronouns correctly.

Use clear antecedents for pronouns.

Incorrect	Correct
The benefits are excellent. They said that I would have six weeks' vacation in five years. (Who are *they*?)	Mr. Bronson assured me that the benefits are excellent. He said. . . *(Mr. Bronson* is the antecedent of *he*)

Use correct pronoun references. A pronoun takes the place of a noun or another pronoun, not an idea.

Incorrect	Correct
The train was delayed, which caused our late arrival.	The train delay caused our late arrival.
I arrived at work at 10:30 AM. This infuriated my employer.	My arrival at work at 10:30 AM infuriated my employer.

Use verbs correctly.

Avoid incorrect shifts in person and number.

Incorrect	Correct
If one (THIRD PERSON) really wants to succeed, you (SECOND PERSON) can do so,	If you (SECOND PERSON) really want to succeed, you (SECOND PERSON) can do so.
Yesterday I (SINGULAR) interviewed Carla Benson, a former employee of yours, and we (PLURAL) were impressed by her skills.	Yesterday I (SINGULAR) interviewed Carla Benson, and I (SINGULAR) was impressed by her skills.

Avoid incorrect shifts in tense.

Incorrect	Correct
Only a single window opened (PAST) onto the street; the back of the house has (PRESENT) generous windows and doors.	Only a single window opens (PRESENT) onto the street; the back of the house has (PRESENT) generous windows and doors.

Avoid incorrect shifts in voice.

Incorrect	Correct
We shipped (ACTIVE) the dishes today, and the glasses will be sent (PASSIVE) next week.	We shipped (ACTIVE) the dishes today, and we will send (ACTIVE) you the glasses next week.

Express appreciation correctly.
Thanking people in advance implies that they must fulfill your request.

Express appreciation in the present tense only after a request has been granted. Use the conditional *should* or *would* to express appreciation before a request has been granted.

Before	After
I should appreciate your sending me. . .	I appreciate your sending me. . .
I would be grateful for the opportunity to discuss this proposal in person.	Thank you for the opportunity to discuss this proposal in person.

Concise

Business writing should be free of nonessential detail, containing only what is necessary for completeness, clarity, and courtesy. Ideas should be expressed in as few words as possible without sacrificing politeness or completeness.

Which of the following would you rather read?

With reference to your recent request for 50 reprints of the article "Time Management" in the May issue of *Modern Management*, these copies are enclosed for your convenience.	Here are the 50 reprints of "Time Management" you requested.

To make your writing concise. . .

Omit unnecessary words and phrases, such as those enclosed in parentheses in the following list.

at (the hour of) six	each (and every)
because (of the fact that)	the (matter of) cost
came (at a time) when	(temporarily) suspended
consensus (of opinion)	(in order) to
during (the course of) the discussion	until (such time as) we can
five (in number) were	cancel (out)
for (the purpose of)	throughout (the year of) 1997
neat (in appearance)	postpone (until later)
his (own) autobiography	penetrate (into)
(falsely) misrepresented	square (in shape)
glance (briefly)	small (in size)
popular (with the people)	reason was (because)
a (free) gift	disappear (from sight)
(future) outlook	(true) facts
(personal) opinion	revert (back)

Eliminate all forms of "to be."

proved (to be) accurate	smaller than we expected (it to be)

Instead of	Say
His hair was black, and his hairline was receding; his deep brown eyes were clear and thoughtful.	His hair was black; his hairline, receding; his eyes, clear and thoughtful.

Use short, natural-sounding words instead of long, indirect expressions.

Instead of	Say
a check in the amount of	a check for
at all times	always
at the present time	now
due to the fact that	because of
during the time that	while
inasmuch as	as
in the event that	if
in view of the fact that	because

I wish to bring to your attention	Please note
previous to, prior to	before
put in an appearance	came
under separate cover	separately

Use a single, strong verb instead of a weak noun/verb combination.

Instead of	Say
made an announcement	announced
came to the conclusion	concluded
gave consideration to	considered
made him a loan	lent
held a meeting	met
raised an objection	objected
made an offer of	offered
placed an order	ordered
gave some thought to	thought about

Avoid indirect expressions. Don't ask permission to make a statement. Express your requests in a polite, direct manner. Avoid the expletives *it* and *there.* Use direct questions rather than indirect ones.

Instead of	Say
May I suggest that you call me to make an appointment.	Please call me to make an appointment.
I wonder whether you can see me on the 17th.	Can you see me on the 17th?
There is the possibility that the Dallas office will be closed.	The Dallas office may be closed.
It was clear to the supervisor on what basis they wanted to promote her.	The supervisor knew why they wanted to promote her.
It is the recommendation of the finance committee that. . .	The finance committee recommends. . .
There is only one objection to your proposal and that is the time it will require.	The only objection to your proposal is the time required.

Use the active voice. To write direct and concise sentences, use the active voice (subject performs the action). The active voice makes writing more vivid, interesting, and concise. The passive voice (subject receives the action) always uses more words.

Passive	Active
Thirty-five minutes can be saved by flying to Mapleton.	You can save 35 minutes by flying to Mapleton.

The passive voice is not incorrect but should be used carefully and deliberately when you do not want to emphasize the doer of the action.

Passive	Active
Your order was mistakenly shipped to another company.	I mistakenly shipped your order to another company.

Effective Business Writing

Simplify clauses and phrases.

Change compound sentences to simple ones.

Compound
We will accept the returned motor, and we will credit your account

Simple
We will accept the returned motor and credit your account.

Change dependent clauses to phrases.

Dependent Clause
Mail the card today so that you will not miss the first issue of *Keynotes*.

Phrase
Mail the card today to avoid missing the first issue of *Keynotes*.

Change dependent clauses to appositives.

Dependent Clause
The No. 5, which is our best grade, sells for $3 a yard.

Appositive
The No. 5, our best grade, sells for $3 a yard.

Change dependent clauses and prepositional phrases to one-word adjectives or adverbial modifiers.

Dependent Clause
We appreciate the suggestions that you sent us.

Adjective
We appreciate your suggestions.

Prepositional Phrases
She spoke with confidence about her plans for the future.

Adverb/ Adjective
She spoke confidently about her future plans.

Don't repeat yourself. Avoid thanking "again" or saying anything else "again." Once is usually enough. Don't repeat what you have already stated clearly.

Courteous

Business writing should be friendly in tone without being too informal. It should also understand the reader's viewpoint, reflect a sincere wish to be helpful, be properly timed, and use language acceptable to everyone.

To achieve a friendly tone...

1. Use natural, conversational words, not bureaucratic or pompous ones.
2. Stress the positive, not the negative.
3. Seek to achieve goals and solve problems, not express annoyance or lay blame.
4. Be straightforward and to the point, not passive and hedging.

Use natural, conversational words.

Instead of
The enclosed material must be redrafted as indicated herein, and the revision submitted to me no later than Thursday next. The final version should be submitted to the board at their meeting on Monday, May 8, if we are to gain their approval.

Say
I've indicated on your report the sections you should revise. If you can send the final draft by next Thursday, I will submit it for approval at the board's May 8 meeting.

Stress the positive, not the negative. Stress what is and what can be. Avoid negative words and phrases such as *claim, failed to, neglected to, lack of.* **You want to motivate your reader, not scold or punish.** Address unpleasant matters without offending; propose actions to improve the situation.

Negative	Positive
These playsuits may fade and shrink if washed in hot water.	Washed in cold water, these playsuits will stay bright and keep their size for the life of the garment.
Our Customer Service Department is not open after 5 PM and on weekends.	Our Customer Service Department is open to help you Monday through Friday from 8:30 to 5.
I am writing regarding your failure to remit payment of your invoice.	Did you receive our bill?
Mr. Golden claims he did not know about the policy cancellation.	Mr. Golden says he did not know about the policy cancellation.
You consistently fail to show up on time.	You must arrive by 8:30 AM.
We cannot deliver your shipment before next week.	We will deliver your shipment next week.

Business letters should have a positive tone whenever possible, but they cannot always avoid negative statements. Denying a request, refusing an invitation, or stating dissatisfaction may actually be the purpose of the letter. Always remember, however, that every letter has the important underlying purpose of creating goodwill and making a favorable impression. In a sentence containing both good and bad news, give the bad news first so that the reader's last thought is a positive one.

Instead of	Say
Enclosed is a $50 check, but I don't have time to serve on your committee.	My schedule, unfortunately, does not permit my serving on your committee, but I am pleased to enclose a $50 check for your worthy cause.
Shopping Tips is still selling well in bookstores, but *Shopping Tips II* will not be ready for fall publication.	Because of editing problems, *Shopping Tips II* will be out in the spring, but *Shopping Tips* is still available in bookstores.

Bury a negative word in the middle of the sentence.

Instead of	Say
Unfortunately, I cannot attend the seminar.	I cannot, unfortunately, attend the seminar.

Bury a negative message in the middle of the letter. In refusing an invitation to be a guest speaker, for instance, use the first paragraph to express appreciation to the reader for having extended the invitation and the last paragraph to wish him or her well with the program.

Be straightforward and to the point, not passive and hedging.

Instead of	Say
The customer should receive the new modem within a few days.	I'm shipping the new modem to the Arco Company tomorrow.
An error seems to have been made by the mailroom staff.	The mailroom staff shipped to the wrong company.

Keep the reader in mind.   Whenever possible, use the pronouns *you* and *your* instead of *I, my, we,* and *our.*

Following this guideline, especially in your first paragraph, will produce reader-centered writing.

Instead of	Say
I was attracted by your advertisement in Sunday's *Boston Globe* for the book *Planning Your Future.*	Your advertisement in Sunday's *Boston Globe* for *Planning Your Future* caught my eye.
I want you to know that your talk on the opportunities available in the legal field was both enjoyable and informative.	Your talk on the opportunities available in the legal field was both enjoyable and informative.
I was glad to find that your report is excellent, as I expected it to be.	Your report is excellent, as I expected it to be.

Be careful to avoid a forced, unnatural opening sentence. Do not start a letter with *you* or *your* if that will produce a stiff, heavy, passive construction. Do start with *I, my, we,* or *our* if doing so is more natural.

Instead of	Say
Your help is needed by us in order to design a new letterhead for our company.	We have decided to give our letterhead a new look and would like you to design it for us.

Show a sincere wish to be helpful by doing more than you have to, to make responding as convenient as possible for your reader.

For example, when you enclose a brochure or catalog, give the page number where the item of interest to the reader is located.

Enclose a form for people to fill in or check off to save their having to write a letter or memo.

Enclose an addressed, stamped envelope, if appropriate, to make responding easier.

Time your response for the best effect.   Promptness is usually a virtue, but if you must deny a request, you may wish to delay the answer for a short time so your reader feels you considered the request fully before denying it.

Use language acceptable to everyone.   Certain compound nouns containing *man* or *men* have traditionally been used to mean both male and female. Many have criticized this practice as being biased against women. Below are some appropriate substitutions.

Instead of	Say
businessmen	business owners, business executives, managers, business people
salesmen	salespeople, sales representatives, salesclerks, sales staff
foremen	supervisors
policemen	police officers
mailmen	mail carriers
congressmen	members of Congress, Congressional members, senators and representatives
manpower	work force
stewardess	airline attendant, flight attendant
authoress, poetess	author, poet

When naming a job or role, avoid the use of a term that signifies a male or female in that role unless you are describing a specific person whose gender is known.

Instead of	Say
Ten are seeking election as councilmen.	Ten candidates are seeking election to the City Council.
Write your Congressman today.	Write your representative in Congress today.
Who was named chairman?	Who was named to chair the committee?

Some companies approve the use of terms like *chairperson* and *spokesperson*; others find such terms somewhat awkward and contrived. Follow personal taste or company policy.

Terms like doctor, lawyer, and nurse apply equally well to men and women. Do not use terms like woman doctor or male nurse unless you have a specific reason for referring to gender.

Not Relevant	Relevant
He was defended by a female attorney.	Male nurses now constitute 20 percent of the profession.

Slang and colloquialisms have no place in business writing.

Complete

Business writing should include all essential information and should be sufficiently detailed to be clear.

Once you understand the principles of good writing, you are ready to put it all together by. . .

Choosing the Right Words

Choose precise, natural-sounding words. Avoid jargon and clichés. Be concise. Use strong verbs and clear pronoun references. Be consistent in number, tense, and voice. Avoid sexist language, colloquialisms, and slang.

Writing Effective Sentences

Effective sentences use the basic techniques of good writing. These techniques will result in unified, concise, logical sentences. In addition, such sentences will be clearly and correctly punctuated and will provide variety in your writing.

Unified sentences express one complete thought or use proper conjunctions or transitional expressions to connect related ideas.

> Yesterday I interviewed Carla Benson, a former employee of your firm.

> Yesterday I interviewed Carla Benson, a former employee of your firm, *and* was impressed by her attitude and her skills.

> She is alert and intelligent; she claims, *however*, that the ability to concentrate is the key to her success.

Pronouns, synonyms, and summary words and phrases also connect sentences and lend variety to a communication.

> **Transitional Pronoun:** Bermuda is a pleasant spot; *it* attracts many visitors.

> **Synonym:** We hope you will enjoy using your new IBM computer. *This machine* has . . .

> **Summary Word:** We suggest that you consider opening schools on the West Coast. *This expansion...*

Use conjunctions correctly to tie ideas together logically and smoothly.

> She enjoys poultry, whereas (contrast) I prefer fish.

> We looked forward to meeting him, but (contrast) he canceled at the last minute.

> While (time) I was in the store, he was at the dry cleaners.

Vary Sentence Structure

Simple: Because of the school's excellent reputation, it attracts many students.

Compound: The school has an excellent reputation, and therefore, it attracts many students.

Complex: The school, which has an excellent reputation, attracts many students.

Degree-Result Clause: *The sooner* you make your reservation, *the more certain* you will be of good accommodations.

Introductory Adverbial Clause: *When you are making your flight reservation,* please specify first-class or tourist.

Prepositional-Gerund Phrase: *By making your reservations now,* you will be assured of first-class accommodations.

Introductory Infinitive Phrase: *To be assured of a flight reservation,* confirm it before noon on Monday.

Participial Absolute Phrase: *Flight reservations being in demand,* we suggest you make your reservations well in advance.

Subordinate Less Important Material

To emphasize that one thought is more important than another, express the more important one in an independent clause and the less important one in a dependent clause, a phrase, or an appositive.

Dependent Clause: *Because Puerto Rico is a wonderful vacation area,* it attracts many visitors.

Appositive: Puerto Rico, *a pleasant vacation area,* attracts many visitors.

Infinitive Phrase: *To attract visitors,* Puerto Rico offers excellent package plans.

Writing Unified Paragraphs

A unified paragraph relates to one aspect of the message; every sentence in the paragraph develops that aspect. Because long paragraphs look formidable to the reader, divide a long paragraph into two paragraphs of three to five sentences each. Be sure to divide at a logical point.

Organizing the Whole

Be aware of the structure of the entire communication. Have a beginning, middle, and end to the presentation. Determine the main point. State the main point in the beginning, and sustain it throughout the communication. Develop the subject in the middle. Summarize it in the end, or recommend a course of action. Be specific and clear. Include transitions. Subordinate the less important material to the more important. Eliminate anything that does not contribute either to the content or the courtesy of the communication.

The beginning, middle, and conclusion of the communication may correspond to the following example:

Beginning: What is the message?

Middle: What do I want to say about the message?

Conclusion: What will I do about the message?
                or
                What do I want my reader to do about the message?

Beginning Section

The opening paragraph is the most important paragraph in a communication. It should tell the reader clearly and concisely what the communication is about.

The opening sentence of the first paragraph should be a strong and positive one. This headline position should never be given to an introductory phrase such as *Answering your inquiry, Acknowledging your letter, In reference to (In response to, Regarding) your letter.* Similarly, the statements *We have received your letter* and *Your letter has been received* are unnecessary since the fact that the letter is being answered is evidence that it was received.

The following phrases are weak and overused:

> Please be advised. . .   Referring to your letter of. . .
> As per your request. . .   Thank you for your letter.
> Enclosed please find. . .   This will acknowledge your letter of. . .
> Attached is. . .   We regret (are pleased) to inform you. . .

Place a necessary reference (as in an order from a repeat customer) to the date of an inquiry in a dependent clause or a phrase.

> Your latest order, dated April 16, will be sent to you early next week.

When the date is unimportant, omit it.

> The Mitsubishi Early American console you ordered will be sent to you early next week.

Middle Section

The middle section of a communication develops the message by providing explanatory or supporting facts. In a lengthy report, there may be a number of paragraphs in the middle section, and these paragraphs will have an order within the larger whole. For instance, chronological order or order of importance might be appropriate to the middle section of a report.

Conclusion

The concluding paragraph of a communication should perform one or more of the following functions:

Briefly summarize the action you expect the reader to take.

> Mrs. Kelly and I should appreciate hearing from you by May 25. Your evaluation will help the Program Committee complete its preparation for the annual board meeting.

Express the action you expect to take.

> If I have not heard from you by June 25, I will call your office to inquire about the status of my application.

Express goodwill.

> Best wishes for success with your seminar.

Make your closing sentence specific to each letter. Avoid clichés.

Instead of	Say
If you need further information, do not hesitate to contact me.	Please call me if you wish to discuss this proposal.

CHAPTER 10 **Model Letters**

CHAPTER 10 # Model Letters

The following are samples of different kinds of typical business letters and memos. A formula is given to guide you through various situations, but remember that each situation is unique and you will need to use an approach that works well for you and your company.

Before you write, you should

1. Know your purpose (Why are you writing this letter? What do you want to achieve? What response do you want?)

2. Know yourself. (Are you an expert, a teacher, a salesperson? Are you justified in giving your opinion? What particular knowledge do you have?)

3. Know your reader. (What is the reader's title, relationship to the writer, training, education, and status? What attitude do I expect the reader to have toward my message?)

Plan Before You Write

1. **Think** about the topic; gather the pertinent facts. Before beginning to write, answer these questions:

> What is the topic? (This should become your opening sentence.)
>
> Who is my reader? (This will help you determine your tone and your level of language.)
>
> What do you want to say about the topic?
> List all essential details: How? When? Where? How much? What time? Who?
>
> What do I want the reader to do next? *or* What am I going to do next? (One of these should become your closing sentence.)

2. **Organize** the facts by numbering them according to the order of their importance.

3. **Write** the first draft, expressing the facts in sentences and paragraphs. Follow the order determined in Step 2. Write quickly and naturally.

4. **Rewrite** according to the principles of effective writing. Edit for tone, transition, emphasis, sense, and vocabulary. If possible, leave some time between writing the first draft and rewriting. Read the work aloud so that you can hear what you have written.

5. **Type** the communication and **proofread** for the following:
   completeness and accuracy of information
   spelling
   punctuation
   style points
   spacing
   general appearance

Never trust spell-check or grammar-check to catch every error.

You may wish to have a second reader proofread the finished work as a final check.

Request for an Item

1. **Give background or reason for request.**

2. **State request specifically, completely, concisely. Use a question or questions if possible.**

3. **Express appreciation without implying an expected favorable response by using the conditional mood. ("I would (should) appreciate. . ." rather than "I appreciate. . . .")**

Reader's Digest
79 Forest Avenue
Wakefield, IL 90452

Dear Sir or Madam:

      Subject: Reprints of the Article " The Changing Face of America"

The theme of our upcoming national conference on June 17-20 is "Staying Competitive in the Global Marketplace." An article in your January 1995 issue, "The Changing Face of America," illustrates precisely the message we want to convey to our employees.

Are reprints available? If so, we would like 100 copies at your regular reprint rate. If no reprints are available, may we make photocopies of the article? The photocopies would be distributed without charge only to our own personnel. Your magazine would be fully credited as the source.

Because we hope to complete our conference plans by May 10, I would appreciate receiving either your permission or the reprints by then.

                Very truly yours,

                Michael Hengel
                Director, Sales Training

MH:lw

Favorable Response

1. **Refer courteously to the request in the opening paragraph, and state what is being done about the request.**

2. **Refer to any material enclosed or being sent separately to the reader.**

3. **Indicate pleasure in being of service, or express good wishes, if appropriate. Do not unnecessarily solicit further contact if you have fulfilled the request.**

Mr. Michael Hengel
Director, Sales Training
Omega Products, Limited
9087 William Street
Brookline, MA 01234

Dear Mr. Hengel:

One hundred reprints of the article "The Changing Face of America," which appeared in our January 1995 issue, are being sent to you by first-class mail.   You should receive them by next week.

We do charge a nominal fee of 50 cents a copy to cover our costs. Enclosed, therefore, is an invoice for $50.

We are always pleased when one of our readers thinks enough of our publication to request the use of one of our articles for business or personal reasons and are happy to contribute, in even a small way, to the success of your conference.

Sincerely,

Mary Manning
Public Relations Director

MM:pw

Enclosure

Unfavorable Response

1. Refer courteously to the request, and express interest in the reader's problem or project.

2. Say in a positive and friendly tone that the request cannot be granted, implying that you would prefer to say "yes."

3. Explain without apology the reason for the refusal.

4. Suggest other sources of assistance if possible.

5. Express good wishes for the success of the reader's objectives.

Mr. Michael Hengel
Director, Sales Training
Omega Products, Limited
9087 William Street
Brookline, MA 01234

Dear Mr. Hengel:

Thank you for your compliments on the article "The Changing Face of America." We are always pleased when our readers request use of our articles for business or personal reasons.

Usually, we are happy to supply reprints for a nominal sum. The author of this article, however, did not give us permission to do so; and therefore we would be violating copyright law if we gave you permission to reproduce this article.

We excerpted this article from the June 1994 issue of *National Observer*, 1500 Jefferson Avenue, NW, Washington, DC 10098; telephone: (201) 788-9076. Susan Ross in the legal department of *National Observer* may be able to grant permission or to put you in touch with the author.

Best wishes on the success of your conference on this important challenge facing American business.

Sincerely,

Mary Manning
Public Relations Director

MM:pw

Request for Information

1. **Give background or reason for request.**

2. **State request specifically, completely, concisely. Use a question or questions if possible.**

3. **Express appreciation without implying an expected favorable response by using the conditional mood. ("I would [should] appreciate....").**

Dr. Anthony D'Angelo
Business English Department
Mannix College
One Center Street
Troy, NY 12579

Dear Dr. D'Angelo:

Your excellent reputation as chairperson of the Business English Department has prompted me to request your help. Would you please recommend an up-to-date book on business English?

Our company does its own desktop publishing, and I do a great deal of proofreading. A reference book that covers punctuation, capitalization, number expression, and usage would help me do my work more quickly and efficiently.

I should appreciate your writing to me at the above address or calling me at (212) 234-9078, Extension 554, with any suggestions you may have.

Sincerely yours,

Toni Morris
Administrative Assistant

TM

Request for Appointment

1. **Identify yourself to the reader unless you are already known.**

2. **State briefly and clearly the purpose of the appointment.**

3. **Suggest possible details of the appointment arrangement, but do not set an exact time. Offer to telephone to learn whether an appointment will be arranged.**

4. **Express the hope of a favorable response.**

Marvin Katzman, Ph.D.
Chairman, Humanities Department
Dealy Hall
Westminster College
Bronx, NY 09765

Dear Dr. Katzman:

I am a freelance writer, currently researching an article for *Newsweek* on the status of liberal arts education in American schools. I believe your views, research, and experience at one of the most prominent liberal arts colleges in New York would add greatly to my understanding of this subject.

I should appreciate your giving me approximately two hours of your time to discuss this topic and would hope that you could also arrange for me to sit in on some classes at Westminster. Would a day during the week of November 11 be convenient for you?

I will call your office early next week to see whether your schedule will permit your participation in my research for this article.

Very truly yours,

Evelyn Morgan

Cancellation of an Appointment

1. Refer courteously to the appointment by date, time, and place.

2. Ask that the appointment be canceled and give the reason for the cancellation.

3. If you wish another appointment, suggest possible dates or offer to follow up with a telephone call to reschedule.

Marvin Katzman, Ph.D.
Chairman, Humanities Department
Dealy Hall
Westminster College
Bronx, NY 09765

Dear Dr. Katzman:

I regret that I will not be able to meet with you on Monday, November 11, at 10 AM in your office, as we previously arranged.   My publisher has scheduled me to speak at an out-of-town conference on that day.

I will be back in New York on Wednesday, November 13. May we reschedule our interview for later that week? I am eager to include your views in the article I am writing for *Newsweek* about the status of liberal arts education in American schools.

I will call your office early next week to see when it might be convenient for you to see me.

Sincerely,

Evelyn Morgan

Request for Reservations

1. Give all specific facts surrounding the reservation: dates, times, number of people, type of accommodations required, etc.

2. Tabulate when feasible.

3. Express appreciation in the conditional mood.

The Stanhope Hotel
Wilson and Main Streets
San Francisco, CA 09987

Attention: Reservations

Dear Sir or Madam:

Our president, Mr. Carl Haas, would like to reserve accommodations at your hotel for the three nights of his stay in San Francisco: Monday, April 4; Tuesday, April 5; and Wednesday, April 6.

Mr. Haas will arrive at the Stanhope on April 4 before 6 PM and will depart on April 7 at noon. He will require a living room and bedroom suite. In addition, he will need the use of a small conference room (15-20 people) on Wednesday, April 6, from 2 until 5 PM.

Please send me the following information:

1. Confirmation of this reservation
2. Cost of the requested accommodations
3. Amount of advance deposit if necessary

Since I need to complete Mr. Haas's itinerary, I would appreciate hearing from you by the 15th.

Sincerely,

John Adams
Secretary

Secretarial Acknowledgment

1. Refer courteously but briefly to the letter received and its contents.

2. Tell why the letter is not being answered by the person to whom it is addressed, being careful not to reveal personal information.

3. Explain what action the writer is taking, but avoid promising what someone else will do unless authorized to do so.

4. Close without personal remarks.

Ms. Roseanne Paik
Marketing Manager
PPPaik Associates, Inc.
90 South Ventura Avenue
West Dover, DE 78543

Dear Ms. Paik:

Your letter to Ms. Nancy Morris, asking for her approval of your design of our fall sales brochure, came at a time when Ms. Morris is attending an international conference in Munich, Germany. She is not expected back in the office for three weeks.

I have forwarded your letter and a copy of the brochure to her. She has said that she will be in touch with you within the next two weeks.

Very truly yours,

Lisa Visentin
Administrative Assistant

Telephone Follow-Up

1. **Repeat information communicated by telephone to provide a permanent record of the conversation.**

2. **Close by stating what needs to happen next in order for the reader to act on this information.**

Mr. and Mrs. Nicholas Pappas
21-79 217th Street
Bayside, NY 11358

Dear Mr. and Mrs. Pappas:

As I explained to you in our phone conversation of Tuesday, January 15, a landlord must resort to the legal process in order to evict a tenant. Failure to follow legal procedures is now considered a misdemeanor in New York State.

If you wish to evict Mr. and Mrs. Jones, you must institute a summary process action in the Supreme Court. If you are successful in this court proceeding, the tenants may leave voluntarily, or you may need to ask the sheriff to evict them.

Should you decide to institute a summary process action, please call me, and I will prepare the necessary papers for you.

Very truly yours,

Donald J. Evans
Attorney at Law

DJE:jn

Order Letter

1. Give precise information about the item(s) being ordered, tabulating if more than one item is involved.

2. Specify the shipping address and any special instructions.

3. Give the method of payment.

Staples, Incorporated
100 Roslyn Road
Canton, OH 87123

Attention: Order Department

Dear Sir or Madam:

Please send the following items to the above address:

Quantity	Catalog No.	Item	Unit Price	Total
100	N237	Maxell MF2hd Floppy Disks	$7.95	$795.00
50	P870	Yellow lined pads	.95	47.50
4	X33	Heavy-duty staple guns	3.95	15.80
25	LT980	Reams laser printer paper	11.50	287.50
			Total	$1,145.80

Please enclose a bill, including sales tax and shipping and handling charges, with your shipment. We would appreciate your sending these items at once.

Sincerely,

Desmond Frankel
Office Manager

DF:PI

Request for Payment

1. **State the problem.**

2. **Express concern about lack of payment.**

3. **Request payment and/or a response.**

Mr. Walter Slomin
Q-Zark Corporation
12 Denton Avenue, NW
Morristown, NJ 67412

Dear Mr. Slomin:

After reviewing our accounts, I find that your payment to us is three months overdue.

Enclosed is a copy of our invoice for the two desks, three chairs, and four bookcases you purchased for your showroom. Are you satisfied with the furniture?

We are concerned because your bill has not been paid and you have not offered us any explanation.

Please telephone me to discuss this matter and to set up a schedule for payment of the $2017.95 you owe us.

Very truly yours,

Harold G. Yorio
Accounting Department

HGY:SW

Enclosures

Collection Letter

1. **State the problem, giving the specifics of the amount due, dates of letters or orders, merchandise purchased, and so forth.**

2. **Present the argument for payment.**

3. **Close with a question specifically asking for payment.**

4. **Be courteous but firm in tone.**

Mr. Walter Slomin
Q-Zark Corporation
12 Denton Avenue, NW
Morristown, NJ 67412

Dear Mr. Slomin:

We wrote to you on September 27 and on October 30, requesting payment of your past-due account of $2017.95 or an explanation of why you have not paid for the office furniture you bought from us.

We are sorry you have not replied because we want to help our customers whenever possible. We filled your order promptly and, we assume, satisfactorily, since you have made no reply to our offer of adjustment.

As you know, our credit terms call for payment within 30 days. Your account is now six months overdue. If we do not hear from you in the next two weeks, we will be obliged to refer your account to our attorney.

Won't you use the enclosed envelope to send us your check?

Very truly yours,

Harold G. Yorio
Accounting Department

HGY:SW

Enclosure

c Frank A. McGee, Esq.

Claim Letter

1. **Include all specific details relevant to the problem.**

2. **Avoid a negative tone.**

3. **If possible, state the desired adjustment.**

4. **Express confidence that the matter will be handled promptly and satisfactorily.**

Pembroke Publishers
1700 Sixth Avenue
Wilton, CT 06098

Attention: Order Department

Dear Sir or Madam:

The copy of *Technology in the Office of the 21st Century*, which I ordered from you on August 15, has not yet arrived. I did, however, receive a bill for it on September 4. Can you explain the delay in my receipt of the book?

The bill, Invoice No. 763286, is dated September 1 and includes the price of the book ($18.95) plus a postage charge of $1.75. I plan to pay the bill as soon as I receive the book.

Because your company has an excellent reputation, I am confident you will trace this order at once and that I will soon receive a copy of *Technology in the Office of the 21st Century*.

Sincerely yours,

Michael Lewis
Office Manager

ML:ws

Apology for Poor Service

1. **Say immediately what you are doing to solve the problem.**

2. **Explain how you think the error came about without specifically naming any individual.**

3. **Apologize and, if possible, make amends to retain the customer's goodwill.**

Mr. Michael Lewis
Office Manager
Fanning Personnel
21 Lancaster Street
Minneapolis, MN 73209

Dear Mr. Edwards:

The book you ordered, *Technology in the Office of the 21st Century*, is being shipped via Federal Express and should be at your office by Friday of this week.

When I investigated the original shipment, I discovered that your copy of this book was sent to another firm.   It's hard to account for such an error, and the only excuse I can offer is that we have had several temporary warehouse workers this summer to replace members of our vacationing crew.

I apologize for this delay and hope that this special shipment will help to compensate for our mistake. Enclosed is a 10 percent discount certificate for you to use the next time you place an order with us.

Sincerely,

Morgan Freehold
Manager, Order Department

MF:re

Enclosure

Social Invitation

1. **Extend invitation including details on when and why event is being held.**

2. **Give all important information: time, place, location, etc.**

3. **End with specific instructions for responding and an expression of goodwill.**

Miss Iris McKay
170 Oakdale Drive
Westport, CT 03456

Dear Miss McKay:

The members of the Social Committee at the Katharine Gibbs School in Norwalk invite you to attend a farewell dinner for Carol Lane on Friday, December 6. Carol has accepted a job in Los Angeles and is moving to the West Coast next month.

We will begin at 5:30 PM with a cocktail hour at the Silvermine Tavern in Norwalk (see enclosed map). For dinner you will be able to choose any item on the regular menu. After dinner we will give Carol a gift from all of us to thank her for making our work so much easier and to wish her success in her new job.

If you can join us, please send a check for $65, payable to Katharine Gibbs School, to Mrs. Ann Mason, treasurer of the Social Committee, by Friday, November 27. I know that Carol would be happy to see you, and I hope you will be with us on December 6.

Sincerely,

Marylou McCann
Director

MM:JN

Enclosure

Acceptance of Social Invitation

1. Accept courteously the invitation in the first paragraph, mentioning the occasion, date, hour, and place.

2. Close by expressing appreciation for invitation.

Mrs. Ann Mason
Treasurer, Social Committee
Katharine Gibbs School
900 Newton Avenue
Norwalk, CT 76509

Dear Mrs. Mason:

I will be delighted to attend the farewell dinner for Carol Lane at 5:30 PM on Friday, December 6, at the Silvermine Tavern. Enclosed is my check for $65 to cover the expenses of this occasion.

Carol is a wonderful person, and I look forward to wishing her the very best in her new job and to seeing all my former colleagues at Gibbs.

Thank you for including me in this special occasion.

Sincerely,

Iris McKay

Enclosure

Declination of Social Invitation

1. **Express appreciation for the invitation, mentioning the date and the occasion.**

2. **Briefly give a reason for the declination and express regret courteously.**

3. **If possible, surround the negative response with positives.**

Ms. Marylou McCann
Director
Katharine Gibbs School
900 Newton Avenue
Norwalk, CT 76509

Dear Mrs. Mason:

Thank you for inviting me to attend the farewell dinner for Carol Lane on December 6. An excellent worker and a fine person, Carol certainly deserves this expression of gratitude.

My present position, which involves a great deal of travel, requires that I be at a conference in Houston, Texas, on that day; however, I am enclosing a check for Carol's gift.

Please express to my former colleagues my disappointment at not being able to join them and give all of them my best wishes.

Sincerely,

Iris McKay

Enclosure

Congratulations

1. **Congratulate the reader. If a new business title and/or company is used in the inside address, do not repeat in the letter.**

2. **Amplify the topic with some specific compliments.**

3. **Express support and goodwill.**

Ms. Deborah Dennis-Ryder
Executive Vice-President
NRA Corporation
2700 South Street
Allentown, PA 87654

Dear Ms. Dennis-Ryder:

Congratulations on your promotion! Your president and the members of the NRA Advisory Board have made an excellent choice.

During the course of our business relationship, I have been impressed by your keen understanding of the market and your ability to analyze today's shifting trends. Conferences with you have always been enjoyable as well as informative.

Your promotion increases my good feelings about NRA, and I wish you the best of luck in your new position.

Sincerely,

Thomas W. Scott
Vice-President

TWS: lyr

Sympathy

Sympathy letters are usually written in longhand. Occasionally, however, an executive may request that such a letter be typed on letterhead stationery. A typed sympathy letter is usually acceptable only when a business acquaintance or the family of the business acquaintance is not well known to the writer.

Since sympathy letters are personal and unique, no formula can be given for writing one.

Mr. Kevin Young
126 Eakins Road
Manhasset, NY 11030

Dear Mr. Young:

In this morning's paper I read with sadness of the death of your father.

I consider myself privileged to have been Tom's colleague for the six years I was employed at Hudson's. His warmth and kindness made working with him a pleasure.

Please accept my sincere expression of sympathy at your loss.

Sincerely,

Jacob Dingus

Letter of Introduction

1. The tone of this letter may be more or less formal, depending on whether this is a business or a social introduction.

2. Include the name of the person being introduced, the reason for the introduction, and appropriate information, business or personal.

3. Express your appreciation as well as that of the person being introduced for any courtesy extended.

Mr. Wilson L. Carmine
Purchasing Manager
Westlyan Department Stores
45 Topeka Street
St. James, IN 09538

Dear Mr. Carmine:

Within the next few weeks, you will be visited by Joanne Timmerman, our new sales representative in southern Indiana. Ms. Timmerman is taking the place of Jack Vargas, who has been promoted to regional director.

Ms. Timmerman is a graduate of the Fashion Institute of Technology. She joined our company in 1990 as a colorist and later moved up to a position in quality control. She has spent the last two years traveling to our plants in the South to inspect and to supervise the manufacture of our sheets and towels. When we needed a new sales representative, we immediately thought of Ms. Timmerman. Her "people" skills are excellent, she is thoroughly familiar with our products, and she is committed, as we all are, to customer service and satisfaction.

Thank you for all the courtesies you extended to Jack in the past. I know you will enjoy working with Joanne just as much. She will call you next week to set up an appointment to meet you.

Sincerely,

Marcia McDowell
National Director of Sales

MM:gh

c Joanne Timmerman

Request for a Reference

1. If time has elapsed since the association of the reader and the writer, identify the relationship.

2. Give the reason for the request. If applying for a position, describe it in as much detail as possible.

3. Supply information about current status, additional education, and work experience; and mention the kind of information the reader may be requested to give.

4. Refer to an enclosed addressed, stamped envelope for the reader's use in replying.

Mr. Jeffrey Daniels
Journalism Department
Fordham University
Bronx, NY 78562

Dear Mr. Daniels:

My experience working on the *Ram* under your supervision taught me most of what I know about the newspaper business—how to write, how to edit, how to meet deadlines, and how to produce a professional, high-quality paper on a shoestring.

Since graduating from Fordham in 1994, I have been working in the advertising department of a well-known publishing company. Now I have the opportunity to apply for a job with a local paper.

May I use your name as a reference?

The job I am applying for is assistant advertising manager of the *Manhasset Press*. It will entail both writing and selling ads.   I think my experience with you will be very important, and I'd appreciate your support if someone should inquire about my experience at Fordham.

Enclosed is a stamped, addressed envelope for you to let me know whether you are willing to recommend me.

Sincerely,

Joseph Dooley

Enclosure

Recommendation

1. Specifically identify the person you are recommending and your relationship to him/her.

2. Discuss the pertinent personal qualities and accomplishments that are the basis of your recommendation.

3. Close without unnecessarily soliciting further contact.

Mrs. Evelyn Cox
Human Resources Director
Dayton-Hudson, Incorporated
1500 Jayson Avenue
Detroit, MI 98043

Dear Mrs. Cox:

My former secretary, Susan Marino, wrote to me last week telling me she had applied for the position of your administrative assistant. I am happy to be able to recommend her to you.

Miss Marino was my private secretary for five years. She has excellent secretarial skills. In addition, she demonstrated initiative, perseverance, and punctuality in carrying out her assignments.

With her intelligence, energy, and pleasant personality, Miss Marino will, I am certain, be an asset to your organization.

Sincerely yours,

Marianne Rogers
Director of Marketing

MR:ko

Application Letter with Résumé

A letter of application for a position should include the following information:

1. Source of information about the position—for example, the name and the date of the newspaper in which the advertisement appeared. It is possible, of course, to write an unsolicited letter to a company in which you are interested..

2. Positive statement of your interest in applying for the position:

> I wish to be considered an applicant for that position.
> Please consider me for that position.
> I am therefore submitting my application for. . .

3. Specific reason(s) for applying for the position (name the specific position).

4. Specific reference to the enclosed résumé, particularly as it explain abilities and experience related to or useful in the work required. Do not merely indicate an interest in the field or a desire to learn more about it.

Refer to personal background: courses taken, training, and experience that would be useful in the position. Briefly interpret or enlarge upon the informa tion in the résumé but do not copy or repeat it.

5. Courteous expression of hope that your qualifications warrant favorable consideration and of your availability for an interview.

Follow one of these procedures to make a response easier:

> a. When a letter is sent to a company address, say that you will telephone to learn whether the reader wishes to interview you.

> b. When the letter is addressed to a local newspaper box number, give your telephone number. (The telephone number is included in the résumé but should be repeated in the letter for the convenience of the reader.)

> c. When a telephone call from the reader would be too expensive or impractical, enclose a self-addressed, stamped envelope.

Application Letter with Résumé

Martha Lee Smith
1822 Center Street
Springdale, CA 94040
714 985-2368

June 21, 19—

Personnel Director
Merrill, Smith & Wilson
1000 Ventura Place
Oakland, CA 94051

Dear Sir or Madam:

My recent completion of a one-year secretarial course and my two years' experience in general office work qualify me, I believe, for the secretary-receptionist position you advertised in the June 20 edition of the *Times Chronicle.*

As you can see from my enclosed résumé, I have just graduated with certification from the Katharine Gibbs Secretarial School. My typing and shorthand skills are good, and I am trained in the use of all the latest office technology, including WordPerfect 6.0. I have completed nearly two years of college courses, maintaining a 3.1 grade point average, and can read and write Spanish. I have always made A's in my English courses.

While in college, I worked 25 hours a week and full-time in the summer at a company that specializes in office computer software. My responsibilities included receptionist duties as well as answering the telephone, filing, and producing simple correspondence. Working in retail sales while in high school taught me how to deal with the public in a courteous and efficient way, even during the Christmas rush!

Please consider me for this position. I will call your office next week to see whether I may talk to you in person about my qualifications.

Very truly yours,

Martha Lee Smith

Enclosure

Résumé

Your résumé provides the complete picture of your educational and professional accomplishments. A well-written résumé will not, of itself, get you the job, but many applicants do not get past even the first screening because of poor résumés.

All résumés should include the following information:

1. Personal identification: your name, address, and telephone number at the top of the résumé.

2. Employment history: all the jobs you have held, listed chronologically from the present to the past. Give the name and address or location of each employer, dates of employment, your job title, and a brief job description and/or a concise summary of your accomplishments.

3. Educational background—a list of all the schools you have attended, including dates attended and degrees earned, in chronological order from the present to the past.

4. Special skills that might be relevant to your job performance or that might attract special notice during the interview.

5. References: State that they are available on request. Names and addresses of references should be typed on a separate sheet of paper and brought to the interview.

Many résumés list "position desired" or "career objective" at the top.

If you have little or no work experience, you may supplement your education with a list of courses taken and skills mastered. List any academic or professional honors and awards and professional associations to which you belong.

Do not include salary requirements or reasons for leaving previous jobs. Save these delicate topics for the interview.

A résumé of one page is best, although difficult to achieve as your experience lengthens. Use straightforward English, not technical jargon. Print the résumé on good quality bond paper that matches that of your application letter. Use bold type, underlining, and spacing to make it as attractive as possible.

Many software packages contain templates for résumés that enable you to fill in your own data in a prescribed format. Your résumé, however, should highlight your strengths. Put education first if you have little experience. Put experience first if you have been working for some time. Select those aspects of your experience that suit the requirements of the job for which you are applying.

Résumé

Martha Lee Smith
1822 Center Street
Springdale, CA 94040
714 985-2368

POSITION: Secretary

EDUCATION:

1995—1996   Katharine Gibbs School, New York, New York
                One-Year Secretarial Program. Certified graduate.

1993—1995   Springdale Community College, Springdale, California
                51 credits toward Associate of Arts degree in English.

1989—1993   Springdale High School, Springdale, California
                National Honor Society. Dean's List every semester.

ABILITIES: Typing—50 words a minute; speedwriting—100 words a minute;

                Knowledge of bookkeeping, filing, WordPerfect 6.0; training in
                business writing, telephone techniques, and operation of fax,
                integrated telephone systems, IBM and compatible computers.
                Reading and writing ability in Spanish. Excellent command of
                written and spoken English.

EXPERIENCE:

1993—1995   Meadowbrook Office Systems, Incorporated
                Springdale, California
                Duties: General office work
                Part-time and summer employment

1992—1993   Macy's, Palo Alto, California
                Duties: Salesclerk
                Part-time employment

SPECIAL
INTERESTS: Playing violin with a professional string orchestra.

REFERENCES: Available on request.

Short Memorandum

Aladdin's Magic Carpet Company

INTEROFFICE MEMORANDUM

To: All Employees   **Date:** April 4, 19—

From: Karla Williams,   **Subject:** Vacation Schedules
Personnel Director

Would all employees who wish to take vacation time during the months of July and August please use the tearoff at the bottom of this memo to submit their requests to Miss Jody Lyons in the Personnel Department before noon on Friday, April 30.

I will attempt to honor all requests. However, where conflicts exist, I will give preference to those who have greatest seniority.

KW:JL

— —

To: **Judy Lyons, Personnel Department**   **Subject:** **Vacation Days**

Name: _____ Department: _____

Vacation Days Desired: _____

Long Memorandum

Aladdin's Magic Carpet Company

INTEROFFICE MEMORANDUM

To:	All Employees— Customer Service Department	**Date:**	April 4, 19—
From:	Roger Arno, President	**Subject:**	Relocation

On Monday, April 30, the Customer Service Department will move to the newly renovated offices on the first floor. I hope that this relocation will be accomplished with a minimum of inconvenience to you and to our clients.

Both the local newspapers and the bulletin board in our lobby will announce the move and the fact that the Customer Service Department will be closed on Monday, April 30. The schedule that follows should enable everyone to provide regular services on the days immediately preceding and following the move.

Schedule for Monday, April 30

AM
8:30—10   All papers and personal belongings packed and locked in files and desk drawers.

10—12   1. Movers transfer furniture to new offices.

2. Employees meet with Tom White, Sales Director, in the second floor conference room.

PM
12—2   Employees' lunch. Sandwiches will be served in the conference room for those employees who wish to stay in for lunch.

2—4:30   Set up personal belongings in new offices. Prepare appointments for Tuesday. Make any necessary phone calls as soon as the lines are connected.

Model Letters

If you foresee any problem with the preceding schedule, please bring it to the attention of Ann Klein, your department head. I know that I can count on your cooperation, and I hope that the bright, spacious new offices will compensate for the inconvenience involved in this relocation.

RA:FV

c Ann Klein

CHAPTER 11 Forms of Address

CHAPTER 11 Forms of Address

Unless a specific title, such as *Professor*, *Senator*, or *Judge* is more appropriate, a courtesy title should be placed before a person's name.

In choosing a courtesy title for a woman, always respect her preference. If the preference is unknown, use *Ms.*

> *Ms.* Marion E. Blake
> Dear *Ms.* Blake

If it is not possible to determine the gender of the addressee, omit a courtesy title in the inside address and in the salutation.

> Meredith T. Riker
> Dear Meredith Riker

The correct salutation varies depending on the situation and the formality you wish to achieve.

Individual(s) (Masc.)	Dear Mr. Clay: Dear Sir: (formal and impersonal) Dear Mr. Clay and Mr. Osborne: Gentlemen: Dear Messrs. Clay and Osborne: (formal)
Individual (Female)	Dear Mrs. Hill: Dear Miss Hill: Dear Ms. Hill: Dear Madam: (formal and impersonal)
Courtesy Title Unknown (Female)	Dear Ms. Hill: Simplified (AMS) style—omit the salutation; use a subject line
Two or more women with different surnames	Dear Miss Hill and Mrs. Adams: Dear Misses Hill and Adams: Dear Mss. Hill and Adams: Dear Mesdames Hill and Adams: (formal)
A man and a woman	Dear Miss Hill and Mr. Clay: Dear Mr. Clay and Miss Hill: Dear Mr. and Mrs. Clay:

Professional Titles	Dear Professor Adams:
	Dear Dr. Pelegano:
	Dear Dr. and Mrs. Marsh:
	Dear Drs. Marsh:
	Dear Drs. John and Alice Marsh:
	Dear Dr. Alice and Mr. Frank Marsh:

Organizations

All Men	Gentlemen:
All Women	Ladies:
	Mesdames: (formal)
Mixed	Gentlemen:
	Dear Sir or Madam:
	Gentlemen and Ladies:
	Ladies and Gentlemen:
	Simplified AMS style—omit the salutation and use a subject line

Persons unknown
(Usually a letter of
recommendation)   To Whom It May Concern:

Complimentary Closings: In everyday business correspondence complimentary closings can be more or less formal to suit your degree of familiarity with the reader.

Conservative	Very truly yours,
Business Letters	Yours very truly,
Semipersonal and	Sincerely yours,
Conservatively	Yours sincerely,
Friendly	Very sincerely yours,
	Yours very sincerely,
	Yours truly,
Personal, Informal	Sincerely,
	Cordially,
	Cordially yours,
	Yours cordially,
Very Formal	Respectfully yours,
	Yours respectfully,
	Very respectfully yours,
	Yours very respectfully,
	Respectfully submitted,

The above very formal closings are used in official letters and in transmitting reports or other communications to superior authorities to indicate special respect.

The following tables show the correct forms of address for persons whose rank, office, educational level, or profession requires a special courtesy title and salutation. Examples of both men and women are given.

For further information *The Social List of Washington, D.C.* is available at most local libraries.

For United States Government information, consult The Department of State, Office of Protocol, Ceremonial Section.

Address state and local protocol questions to the governor's office in each state capital and to the mayor's office locally.

Government Officials

Title	Business Address	Social Address
The President of the United States	The President The White House Office Address	The President and Mrs. Smith The White House Home Address
Former President	The Honorable Thomas S. Gilroy Office Address	The Honorable Thomas S. Gilroy and Mrs. Gilroy Home Address
The Vice President of the United States	The Vice President Office Address	The Vice President and Mrs. Smith The Vice President's House Home Address
The Chief Justice	The Chief Justice The Supreme Court Office Address	The Chief Justice and Mrs. White Home Address

Associate Justice (male and female)	Justice Marlboro
	The Supreme Court
	Office Address
		Justice Marlboro and
		  Mrs. Marlboro
		Justice Marlboro and
		  Mr. John Marlboro
		Home Address

Cabinet Member	The Honorable Joseph Cirrito The Secretary of the Interior The Department of the Interior Office Address	The Honorable The Secretary of the Interior and Mrs. Cirrito Home Address

The Attorney General	The Honorable
	Carol Martone
	The Attorney General
	  of the United States
	The Department of Justice
	Office Address
		The Honorable
		The Attorney General
		  and Mr. Peter Martone
		Home Address

Address questions regarding military protocol to each branch of military located nearest you. You can find telephone numbers in your local directory.

To inquire about further information on United Nations protocol, call the United Nations Office of Protocol in New York.

Salutation/Closing	Speaking to/Introducing
Dear Mr. President:	Mr. President or Sir
Most respectfully, Very truly yours,	The President The President of the United States
Dear Mr. Gilroy:	Mr. Gilroy or Sir
Very truly yours, Sincerely yours,	The Honorable Thomas S. Gilroy Former President of the United States
Dear Mr. Vice President:	Mr. Vice President or Sir
Very truly yours, Sincerely yours,	The Vice President of the United States
Dear Mr. Chief Justice:	Mr. Justice White Mr. Chief Justice or Sir
Very truly yours, Sincerely yours,	The Chief Justice
Dear Justice Marlboro Dear Mr. Justice: Dear Madam Justice:/	Justice Marlboro Mr. (Madam) Justice Sir or Madam
Sincerely yours,	Justice Marlboro
Dear Mr. Secretary:	Mr. Secretary or Sir
Very truly yours, Sincerely yours,	Secretary of the Interior, Joseph Cirrito
Dear Madam Attorney General:	Madam Attorney General or Ma'am
Very truly yours, Sincerely yours,	The Attorney General Carol Martone

Title	Business Address	Social Address
Deputy Secretary of the Cabinet	The Honorable Harold Blackman Deputy Secretary of State Department of State Office Address	The Honorable Deputy Secretary of State and Mrs. Blackman Home Address
Speaker of the House of Representatives	The Honorable Francis J. O'Leary The Speaker of the House of Representatives United States Capitol Office Address	The Speaker of the House of Representatives and Mrs. O'Leary Home Address
United States Senator	The Honorable Adam L. Weiss United States Senate Senate Office Building Office Address	The Honorable Adam L. Weiss and Mrs. Weiss Home Address
United States Representative	The Honorable Lisa M. Rocklein House of Representatives House Office Building Office Address	The Honorable Lisa M. Rocklein and Mr. Gary Rocklein Home Address
United States Representative to the United Nations	The Honorable Rockland P. Morris The United States Representative to the United Nations United Nations Plaza Office Address	The Honorable The United States Representative to the United Nations and Mrs. Morris Home Address
American Ambassador	The Honorable Serena J. King The American Ambassador American Embassy Office Address	The Honorable The Ambassador of the United States of America and Mr. Peter L. King Home Address
American Chargé d'Affaires, Consul General	The Honorable Charles P. Gilhooley American Consul General Office Address	The Honorable Charles P. Gilhooley and Mrs. Gilhooley Home Address
United Nations Secretary General	His Excellency The Secretary General of the United Nations United Nations Plaza Office Address	His Excellency The Secretary General of the United Nations and Mrs. Kelly Home Address

Salutation/Closing	Speaking to/Introduction
Dear Mr. Deputy Secretary: Very truly yours, Sincerely yours,	Mr. Deputy Secretary or Sir Deputy Secretary of State, Harold Blackman
Dear Mr. Speaker: Very truly yours, Sincerely yours,	Mr. Speaker or Sir: The Speaker of the House of Representatives, Francis J. O'Leary
Dear Senator Weiss: Very truly yours, Sincerely yours,	Senator Weiss or Sir Senator Adam Weiss from Iowa
Dear Ms. Rocklein: Very truly yours, Sincerely yours,	Ms. Rocklein Representative Lisa Rocklein, from New York
Dear Mr. Ambassador: Very truly yours, Sincerely yours,	Ambassador or Sir The United States Representative to the United Nations Rockland P. Morris
Dear Madam Ambassador: Very truly yours, Sincerely yours,	Madam Ambassador The American Ambassador, Serena J. King
Dear Mr. Gilhooley: Very truly yours, Sincerely yours,	Mr. Gilhooley Mr. Charles Gilhooley
Dear Mr. Secretary General: Very truly yours, Sincerely yours,	Mr. Secretary General or Sir: The Sec. Gen. of the United Nations, His Excellency, Sean Kelly

Title	Business Address	Social Address
Foreign Ambassador	Her Excellency Maria M. Torres The Ambassador of Brazil Office Address	Her Excellency The Ambassador of Brazil and Mr. Ricardo Torres Home Address
Governor	The Honorable Christine T. Royce The Governor of Connecticut Office Address	The Honorable The Governor of Connecticut and Mr. Richard Royce Home Address
State Senator Representative Assemblyman	The Honorable Matthew R. Naclerio Office Address	The Honorable Matthew R. Naclerio and Mrs. Naclerio Home Address
Mayor	The Honorable Edwina B. Olsen Mayor of New York City Hall Office Address	The Honorable Edwina B. Olsen Home Address

Judge	The Honorable
	Warner J. LaRue
	Justice, Appellate Division
	Supreme Court of
	  the State of New York
	Office Address
		The Honorable
		Warner J. LaRue
		  and Mrs. LaRue
		Home Address

Business Professionals

Title	Business Address	Social Address
Attorney	Mary L. Dugan, Esq. or Ms. Mary L. Dugan Attorney at Law Office Address	Mr. and Mrs. Dennis Dugan Home Address
Doctor	Dr. Mary U. Healy or Mary U. Healy, M.D. Office Address	Dr. Mary and Mr. Marvin Healy Home Address
University President	Dr. Paul K. Caginalp President Harvard University Office Address	Dr. and Mrs. Paul Caginalp Home Address

Salutation/Closing	Speaking to/Introducing
Excellency: Dear Madam Ambassador: Sincerely yours,	Madam Ambassador Excellency The Ambassador of Brazil, Maria Torres
Dear Governor Royce: Very truly yours, Sincerely yours,	Governor Governor Royce Ma'am Governor Christine T. Royce of Connecticut
Dear Mr. Naclerio: Very truly yours, Sincerely yours,	Mr. Naclerio Mr. Matthew Naclerio
Dear Mayor Olsen: Dear Madam Mayor: Very truly yours, Sincerely yours,	Mayor Olsen Madam Mayor Mayor Edwina Olsen of New York
Dear Mr. Justice: Dear Justice LaRue: Very truly yours, Sincerely yours,	Mr. Justice Judge LaRue Justice LaRue Judge Warner LaRue

Salutation/Closing	Speaking to/Introducing
Dear Ms. Dugan: Sincerely yours,	Ms. Dugan Ms. Mary Dugan
Dear Dr. Healy: Sincerely yours,	Dr. Healy Dr. Mary Healy
Dear Dr. Caginalp: Sincerely yours,	Dr. Caginalp Dr. Paul Caginalp

Title	Business Address	Social Address
Dean	Dr. Joanne Corti College of Business Administration Yale University Office Address	Dr. Joanne Corti and Mr. Robert Corti Home Address
Professor	Professor Reuben Cohen Department of Economics University of Maine Office Address	Professor and Mrs. Reuben Cohen Home Address

Military Personnel

Title	Business Address	Social Address
Joint Chiefs of Staff Chairman	General Michael Kenny The Chairman of the Joint Chiefs of Staff The Pentagon Office Address	General and Mrs. Michael Kenny Home Address
Chief of Staff, U.S. Army	General Steven Martocci The Chief of Staff of the Army The Pentagon Office Address	General and Mrs. Steven Martocci Home Address
Chief of Naval Operations	Admiral Thomas Wolinski Chief of Naval Operations Navy Department Office Address	Admiral and Mrs. Thomas Wolinski Home Address
Chief of Staff, U.S. Air Force	General Justin Lawrence The Chief of Staff of the Air Force United States Air Force The Pentagon Office Address	General and Mrs. Justin Lawrence Home Address
Commandant of the Marine Corps	General Peter T. Maino The Commandant of the Marine Corps United States Marine Corp Headquarters, U.S. Marine Corp Office Address	General and Mrs. Peter T. Maino Home Address
The Army The Air Force The Marine Corps	Title (Full Name) Branch of Service Office Address	Title (Full Name) and Mrs. (Surname) Home Address

Salutation/Closing	Speaking to/Introducing
Dear Dr. Corti: Sincerely yours,	Dr. Corti Dr. Joanne Corti
Dear Professor Cohen: Sincerely yours,	Professor Cohen Professor Reuben Cohen

Salutation/ Closing	Speaking to/Introducing
Dear General Kenny: Very truly yours, Sincerely yours,	General Kenny General Kenny, Chairman of the Joint Chiefs of Staff
Dear General Martocci: Very truly yours, Sincerely yours,	General Martocci General Martocci, Chief of Staff of the Army
Dear Admiral Wolinski: Very truly yours, Sincerely yours,	Admiral Wolinski Admiral Wolinski, Chief of Naval Operations
Dear General Lawrence: Very truly yours, Sincerely yours,	General Lawrence General Lawrence, Chief of Staff of the Air Force
Dear General Maino: Very truly yours, Sincerely yours,	General Maino General Maino, Commandant of the Marine Corps
Dear Title (Surname): Very truly yours, Sincerely yours.	Title (Surname) Title (Surname)

Title	Business Address	Social Address
The Navy **The Coast Guard**	Title (Full Name) Branch of Service Office Address	Title (Full Name) and Mr. (Full Name) Home Address
United States **Military Academies**	Cadet Christine Allen Company F-5, USCC West Point, NY (zip) Cadet Eric Poto United States Air Force Academy Colorado Springs, CO (zip) Midshipman Rebecca Wolfe United States Merchant Marine Academy Kings Point, NY (zip) Cadet 2/c Laurence Chan United States Coast Guard Academy New London, CT (zip)	

Religious Dignitaries

Title	Business Address	Social Address
Roman Catholic **The Pope**	His Holiness, The Pope or His Holiness, Pope William III Vatican City Address	
Cardinal	His Eminence, Francis Cardinal Blake Archbishop of Chicago Address	
Bishop and **Archbishop**	The Most Reverend Patrick O'Keefe, D.D. Bishop (Archbishop) of Toronto Address	
Priest	The Reverend Father Joshua L. Wilkins Address	
Brother/Sister	Brother John Lee Sister Jan Jaicks Address	

Salutation/Closing	Speaking to/Introduction
Dear Title (Surname):	Title (Surname)
Very truly yours, Sincerely yours,	Title (Surname)
Dear Cadet Allen: Sincerely yours,	Cadet Allen Ms. or Miss Allen
Dear Cadet Poto: Sincerely yours,	Cadet Allen Cadet Poto Mr. Poto
Dear Midshipman Wolfe: Sincerely yours,	Cadet Poto Midshipman Wolfe Ms. or Miss Wolfe
Dear Cadet Chan: Sincerely yours,	Midshipman Wolfe Cadet Chan Mr. Chan Cadet Chan

Salutation/Closing	Speaking to/Introducing
Your Holiness: Most Holy Father: Respectfully yours, Your Holiness's most humble servant,	Your Holiness Most Holy Father His Holiness The Holy Father The Pope The Pontiff
Your Eminence: Dear Cardinal Blake: Respectfully,	Your Eminence Cardinal Blake His Eminence, Cardinal Blake
Your Excellency: Dear Bishop O'Keefe: Respectfully,	Your Excellency Bishop O'Keefe His Excellency, Bishop O'Keefe
Dear Father Wilkins: Respectfully,	Father Wilkins Father Wilkins
Dear Brother John: Dear Sister Jan: Dear Brother/Sister: Respectfully,	Brother Lee; Brother Sister Joan; Sister

Title	Business Address	Social Address
Eastern Orthodox Patriarch	His Holiness, the Ecumenical Patriarch of Constantinople Istanbul, Turkey	
Archbishop	The Most Reverend Michael Archbishop of Miami Address	
Priest	The Very Reverend James Troulakis Address	
Jewish Rabbi with degree Without degree— eliminate letters	Rabbi Aaron Levy, D.D., LL.D. Temple Beth Shalom Address	Rabbi (or Dr.) and Mrs. Levy Home Address
Cantor	Cantor Chaim Potok Temple Beth David Address	Cantor and Mrs. Chaim Potok Home Address
Protestant Clergyman (Without degree— eliminate letters and address as Mr.)	The Reverend John Arluck, D.D.	The Reverend Dr. and Mrs. John Arluck Home Address
Presiding Bishop of the Episcopal Church	The Most Reverend Lee Killian, D.D. Presiding Bishop Office Address	The Most Reverend and Mrs. Lee Killian Home Address
Bishop of the Episcopal Church	The Right Reverend Dorothy Deleston, D.D. Bishop of Iowa Office Address	The Right Reverend and Mr. John Deleston Home Address
Dean	The Very Reverend Shaun Glasco, D.D. Dean of St. Luke's Cathedral Office Address	The Very Reverend and Mrs. Shaun Glasco Home Address
Archdeacon	The Venerable Paul Adam Archdeacon of Madison Office Address	The Venerable and Mrs. Paul Adam Home Address

Salutation/Closing	Speaking to/Introducing
Your All Holiness:	Your All Holiness
Respectfully yours,	His All Holiness
Your Eminence:	Your Eminence
Respectfully yours,	His Eminence
Dear Father Troulakis:	Father
Respectfully yours,	Father Troulakis
Dear Rabbi Cohen:	Rabbi Cohen
Dear Dr. Cohen:	Rabbi
Sincerely yours,	Rabbi Aaron Cohen
Dear Cantor Potok:	Cantor Potok
Sincerely yours,	Cantor Chaim Potok
Dear Dr. Arluck:	Dr. Arluck
Sincerely yours,	The Reverend Dr. Arluck
Dear Dr. Killian:	Bishop Killian
Sincerely yours,	The Most Reverend Lee Killian, Presiding Bishop of the Episcopal Church
Dear Dr. Deleston:	Bishop Deleston
Sincerely yours,	The Right Reverend Dorothy Deleston, Bishop of Iowa
Dear Dean Glasco:	Dean Glasco
Sincerely yours,	The Very Reverend Shaun Glasco, Dean of St. Luke's Cathedral
Dear Archdeacon Adam:	Archdeacon Adam
Sincerely yours	The Venerable Paul Adam, Archdeacon of Madison

CHAPTER 12 **Proofreading**

CHAPTER 12 **Proofreading**

Proofreading requires checking a manuscript for grammar, spelling, punctuation, consistency of style, and factual accuracy. It may involve moving or rewriting entire sentences and paragraphs. To do a good job, you need a firm grasp of English grammar, style, and usage and a strong sense of organizational logic.

You should also have on hand a good dictionary, a thesaurus, and a style manual. Your company may publish its own style manual, or you can use a book such as this one.

Preliminary proofreading should be done right on your computer screen with the help of any software you may have available. A final check should always be done on the printed copy. The more complicated and important the material, the more likely it is that you will have to print it out in order to proof it. When proofreading on paper, use a ruler, an index card, or a sheet of paper to keep your eye focused on one line at a time. Train yourself to read word by word, even character by character, so as not to overlook any errors.

Although software is available that offers a variety of checking features, this aid is far from completely reliable.

For example, it will not distinguish *their* from *there*. Further, any misspelling that is a real word will not be picked up. If a word is spelled too incorrectly, the computer won't include the correct choice as an option, so you'll have to look it up some other way. In addition, the computer will not pick up words that have been accidentally typed twice or hyphens incorrectly left behind when something else has been moved. When you add to or delete from the copy, you have to check that everything still lines up and nothing has jumped from one column to another.

No computer will pick up the wrong date or the wrong address or the wrong amount of money. Spell-check also labels as wrong all kinds of words, names, abbreviations, and so forth, that it is not programmed for. Be especially alert for computer-caused errors: unintentional deletions; italics, boldface, and underlining that run past where they should; or material not properly deleted after it has been moved to another place.

In other words, nothing takes the place of a skilled, thinking person who is proofreading every piece of work.

Think about all of the following when you proofread:

organization	dates and day-date combinations
logical paragraphs	alphabetical order, when appropriate
similar words (*it/if/is*)	cross-references
homonyms (*there/their/they're*)	margins and general appearance
proper nouns	horizontal and vertical alignment
grammatically parallel lists	end-of-line word division
subject/verb agreement	correct page numbers
numbered sequences	heading and captions

punctuation, especially paired punctuation marks
consistent capitalization, particularly in headings, unusual terms, lists, and tables
unintentional repetition of small words (*and, and; the, the*)

Check that the dateline, subject line, initials, enclosure and copy notations have been included.

Check that the table of contents is accurate as to both titles and page numbers.

Check <u>twice</u> any numbers used. Use a calculator to check any mathematical calculations.

Correction Marks for Typed Rough Drafts and Revisions

Mark	Meaning	Mark	Meaning
∧	Make correction indicated in margin.	w.f.	Wrong font; change to proper font.
Stet	Retain crossed-out word or letter; let it stand.	Qu?	Is this right?
....	Retain words under which dots appear; write "Stet" in margin.	lc	Put in lowercase.
✗	Appears battered; examine.	s.c.	Put in small capitals.
✓	Unevenly spaced; correct spacing.	uc	Put in capitals.
//	Line up; i.e., make lines even.	≡	Under letter or word, means caps (capitals).
run in, No ¶	Make no break in the reading; no paragraph.	C+s.c.	Put in caps and small caps.
out see copy	Here is an omission; see copy.	rom	Change to roman.
¶	Make a paragraph here.	ital	Change to italic.
tr	Transpose words or letters as indicated.	=	Under letter or word, means small caps.
⌐	Take out matter indicated; delete.	—	Under letter or word, means italic.
℥	Take out character indicated and close up.	～～	Under letter or word, means boldface.
⌀	Line drawn through a cap means lowercase.	⌄	Insert comma.
⌐⌐	Upside down; reverse.	⌃;	Insert semicolon.
⌣	Close up; no space.	⌃:	Insert colon.
#	Insert a space here.	⊙	Insert period.
⊥	Push down this space.	/?/	Insert question mark.
⊓	Indent line one em.	/!/	Insert exclamation mark.
⊏	Move this to the left.	=	Insert hyphen.
⊐	Move this to the right.	⌄	Insert apostrophe.
⊓	Raise to proper position.	⌄⌄	Insert quotation marks.
⊔	Lower to proper position.	⌄	Insert superior letter or figure.
⊥/M	One-em dash.	⌃n	Insert inferior letter or figure.
⊥/M	Two-em parallel dash.	[/]	Insert brackets.
///	Hair space letters.	(/)	Insert parentheses.

Following is an illustration of a proofread page. Notice how many errors remain even after spell-check has been used.
(In formal proofreading each error must be marked both where it occurs and in the margin immediately to the left or right.)

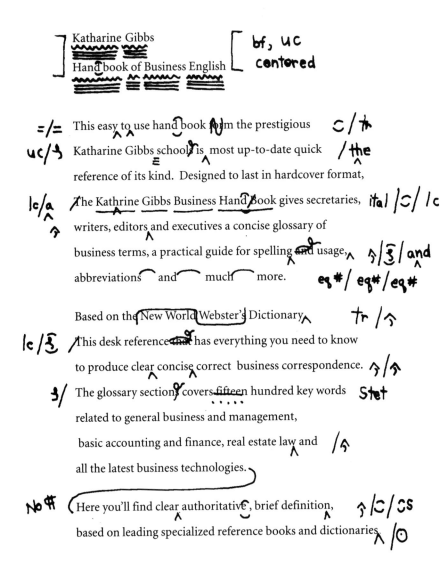

Glossary of Commonly Mistaken Words

A

a
about
above
above all
absolve from
abstain from
accede to
accept
accompanied by
accordingly
according to
account
acquiesce
acquit
across
adapt
adept
adopt
adverse
advice
advise
affect
after
against
aggravate
agree
agreeable to
ahead of
along
along with
all
all of
allot
all ready
all right
all together
allusion
all ways
almost
along with
a lot

already
alright
also
although
altogether
alumna
alumnae
alumni
alumnus
always
am
amid
among
amount
analogous to
and
and etc.
and not
and so forth
an
angry
another
a number
anxious
any
anybody
anymore
anyone, any one
anyone else
anyplace
anything
any time
anyway, any way
anywhere
anywheres
apart from
apiece, a piece
apply
appraise
appreciation of
appreciative of
apprise

aptitude for
apt to
argue
around
as
as a result
as...as
ascent
aside from
as long as
assent
as soon as
assure
as to
as well as
at
at an early date
at any rate
at variance with
at your convenience
authority
avenue
averse
aversion to
awhile, a while

B

bad
badly
balance
be
because
because of
been
before
behind
being
being as, being that
below
beneath
beside
besides
be sure to

between
beyond
biannual
biennial
bimonthly
both
both...and
boulevard
bring
building
but
but not
by
by means of
by reason of
by return mail
by the way

C

can
cannot
can't hardly, can't scarcely
capacity
capital
capitol, Capitol
cite
coincident with
come
company
compare
compatible with
complement
compliment
compliments
comply with
concerning
concur
conducive to
confer
conform to
connect with
consensus
consequently
consul
contact
continually
continuously
contrary to
contrast
convenient
conversant with
corporation

correspond
could
could have
council
counsel
court
credible
creditable

D

data
deficient in
dependent on
descend
descent
desist from
despite
despite the fact that
deter from
devoid of
did
differ
different
different from
differently
dissuaded from
disappointed
disburse
disinterested
disperse
dissent
do
does
done
do not hesitate to...
don't
drive
due to
during

E

each
each one
each other
eager
effect
e.g.
either
either...or
elicit
emigrate
eminent

enclosed
ensure
entrust
envelop
envelope
equally as
especially
Esq.
etc.
even
even if
even though
everyday
every day
everyone
every one
everything
ex-
exactly
except
except for
except for the fact that

F

farther
few
fewer
finally
first
for
foreword
for instance
for the sale of
fortunately
forward
formally
former
formerly
from
further
furthermore

G

gentlemen
go
good
got
graduate from

H

had
hardly

has
have
healthful
healthy
hence
herself
himself
Honorable
hopefully
how
however
however many, few

I
identical with
i.e.
if
illusion
illicit
immanent
imminent
immigrate
imply
in
in accordance with
in addition
in addition to
inasmuch as
in case that
in the near future
including
inclusive
in compliance with
in conformity with
incongruous with
in connection with
incorporated
independent of
indifferent to
in due time
in fact
infer
inferior to
inform
ingenious
ingenuous
in order that
in other words
in place of
in reference to
in regard to
inside

in spite of
in spite of the fact
instead of
instill into
in summary
interested in
into, in to
in view of
irregardless
irrespective of
irritate
insure
is
it
its, it's
itself

J-K
Jr.
just
kind of

L
lane
last
late
latest
latter
lay
lead
leave
led
lend
less
lesser
let
liable to
lie
like
likely to
likewise
limited
loan
loose
lose
loss
ly adverbs

M
makeup, make up
manufacturers
manufacturing

many
may
maybe, may be
meantime
meanwhile
media
merely
Messrs.
might
minus
Miss
Misses
Mmes.
monopoly of
more important
more importantly
moreover
most
Mr.
Mrs.
Ms.
Mss.
much
must
myself

N
near
nearly
necessity
need
negligent
neither
neither..nor...
never
nevertheless
nobody, no body
no doubt
no less than
no matter how
none
no one
nor
not
not only...but also...
notwithstanding
now that
number

O
oblivious
obviously

occasion
of
of course
off
on
on account of
once
on condition that
one
one another
only
only to (verb) that
on the other hand
on the whole
onto, on to
opposite
or
other
otherwise
ourselves
out
out of
outside
over
owing to

P

paid

particularly
passed
past
per
perfect
perhaps
persistent
personal
personnel
pertaining to
place
plan to
plus
possibly
precede
preferably
preparatory to
prerequisite to
principal
principle
prior
prior to
probably

proceed
proved
proven
provided
provided that
providing

Q

quiet
quite

R

raise
rather than
real
really
reason is that
recommend
relating to
refer
referring to
regarding
regardless of
regardless of what
relating to
relative to
respectfully
respectively
retroactive
Reverend
rise
road

S

said
same
scarcely
seldom
semiannual, semimonthly
serve
service
set
several
shall
should
sic
sight
since
sit
site
so
so...as

so that
so...that
some
somebody
someday
some day
someone
some one
someone else
something
sometime
some time
sometimes
somewhere
sort of
speak
square
Sr.
stationary
stationery
still
street
sure
surely

T

take
talk
than
that
their
theirs
themselves
then
the number
there
therefore
there's
these
they're
this
those
through
throughout
thus
till
to
to be sure
to say the least
together with
too
toward

type of
typically

U
under
underneath
under separate cover
(the) undersigned
unfortunately
uninterested
unique
universal
unless
unlike
until
up
upon
used to

V-W
via
vice-

was
way
ways
weather
well
were
what
whatever
when
whenever
where
whereas
whether
whether or not
which
whichever
while
who
whoever
whom
whomever

who's
whose
whosoever
why
will
with
within
with respect to
without
worthy of
would

Y-Z
yet
yet not
your
you're
yourself, yourselves
ZIP Code

Index

Italic type indicates entries in the Glossary of Usage.

I

transitive/intransitive, 75-76
troublesome, 76
Voice, 75, 179, 181
Voting results, 22

W

Way/ways, 153
Weather, 153
Weights, number usage in, 22-23
Well, 144
Whereas, 134
Whether, 145, 153
Which/that, 53, 84, 85
While, 134
Who/whom, 84-85
Will, 151
Words
    choice of for business writing,
        175-76, 180-81, 182-83
    commonly mistaken, 243-47

compound, 119-28
end-of-line division, 127-28
hyphenated, 6, 23
introductory, 52
shortened, 31
summary, 59
unnecessary, 180
as words, plural of, 111
Would, 151
Writing. *See* Business writing;
    Letter writing

Y

Years, 22
You, 184
You're/your, 154

Z

ZIP codes, 15, 29

Notes

Notes

Notes

Spelling

Notes

B.C.

65

90

85

52

- Login Name
- ~~Maritia cepeda~~
  mcepeda

- password
  mcepeda

- confirm password
  mcepeda

Type in the Question
what is my email
address

answer
  mcepeda

company Id
swet54